The talented Yours team, headed by Features Director Caroline, have been painting the Forth Road Bridge again. Their equivalent anyway – the Yours Year Book. Just like the Forth Road Bridge – which starts being repainted one end as soon as they finish at the other – the 2008 Year Book will no sooner be on sale than Caroline will be thinking about what to put into 2009.

Of course the great thing is her army of helpers are all Yours readers sending in wonderful stories and memories to make the Year Book the wonderful keepsake that it is. So, I hope you once again enjoy this Yearbook – and get your paintbrushes primed for 2009!

Best wishes,

Valery

Valery McConnell
Editor, **Yours**

I say it every year but once again the stories you sent in for this year's Year Book have been absolutely cracking and it's been a pleasure to read every single one of them.

Memories so vivid that I tiptoed out with you in the dark to the dreaded outside toilet of your Childhood Home and I was with you paddling in the sea during your Grand Day Out. So many wonderful memories – heartfelt thanks to you all, including those who didn't make it in.

I hope you enjoy dipping into this book throughout the year… there are cities and villages to explore, a wonderful selection of plants and flowers to discover, recipes, reader stories and lots more…

Happy reading during 2008.

Caroline

Caroline Chadderton
Features Director, **Yours**

January 2008

Tuesday

I
Yours magazine on sale
New Year's Day Bank Holiday

Wednesday

2

Thursday

3

Friday

4

Saturday

5

Sunday

6
Epiphany

Monday

7

Tuesday

8

Wednesday

9

Thursday

IO

Friday

II

Saturday

I2

Sunday

I3

Monday

I4

Tuesday

I5
Yours magazine on sale

Wednesday

I6

Thursday

I7

Friday

I8

Saturday

I9

Sunday

2O

Monday

2I

Tuesday

22

Wednesday

23
....

Thursday

24
....

Friday

25
Burns' Night
....

Saturday

26
....

Sunday

27
Holocaust Memorial Day
....

Monday

28
....

Tuesday

29
Yours magazine on sale
....

Wednesday

30
....

Thursday

31
....

PIC: REX FEATURES

Born this month

King of rock ' n' roll, Elvis Presley was born on January 8, 1935 in Tupelo, Mississipi. Elvis was one of twins but his brother, Jesse Garon Presley died at birth.

Married this month

Romantic leading man, Paul Newman (pictured) married award-winning actress and producer Joanne Woodward on January 29, 1958 in Las Vegas. This month they'll be celebrating their golden wedding anniversary!

Died this month

English crime writer Dame Agatha Christie, died on January 12, 1976 at the age of 85. She left a rumoured multi-million pound fortune.

My childhood home

We didn't realise how lucky we were to have been allocated the old lodge house near Keele Hall in North Staffordshire. My Dad was stationed there as a police constable between 1938 and 1950.

I was born on a bitter January night in 1941. The American forces were occupying the mansion at the time and would take turns in the sentry box opposite our front door. As I became a toddler, the pillars of our porch were useful for hiding behind them when the soldiers sang 'Margie' to me.

When the military left in 1945, we had the estate - with its lakes, statues and garden - as our playground.

The woods extended almost to our back door, with a crystal clear stream which gave us watercress.

The lodge became a sanctuary for many animals. A toad would wander in and warm himself by the range in the living room while a shrew would collect the crumbs from under the table and take them back to her hole by the door.

Mum made a stand when the woods had to be cut down in 1949 - Keele Hall was to become a university and playing fields were needed. She bravely placed herself in front of the bull-dozers and refused to budge. They called Dad, who had to carry her in. Thankfully, he didn't arrest her.

It was a terrible day when we had to leave the lodge.

Margaret Horton, Caerphilly

Above: Margaret, her mum, cousin Alan and Rover on the terrace of Keele Hall
Left: The lodge house, Keele

▮ AROUND THE HOUSE ▮

Recycle your Christmas cards by cutting them up for Christmas present labels. Cut out with pinking shears, punch a hole in the corner and thread with string saved from Christmas presents.

Great gardening

Flowers in January? Yes, it's possible

Although most early flowering plants have minuscule (though often extremely well-scented) flowers, such as sarcoccoca, there is one plant that will add both colour and scent to the garden - the cheery hyacinth. Under natural conditions, hyacinths flower in spring but growers now tweak nature by heat treating the bulbs so they bloom in January. It's worth it because hyacinths have such a powefully sweet scent you won't need artificial air freshener for weeks! And, if you want to grow your own early-flowering hyacinths next January, buy prepared bulbs from garden centres in September. Less dark in colour but more widely available is 'Kronos' (below) which you can order from Van Meuwen. Visit www.vanmeuwen.co.uk

▮ TOP TIP ▮

When you store away Christmas decorations put a sheet of fabric conditioner in with them. So next time you unpack them, they'll smell nice, as well as look nice. **Susan Carr, Cleveleys, Lancs**

In the kitchen

CHOCOLATE AND CRANBERRY COOKIES

Makes 12

- 125 g (4 ½ oz) unsalted butter
- 125 g (4 ½ oz) light muscovado sugar
- 2 medium eggs, lightly beaten
- 2 teaspoons vanilla extract
- 225 g (8 oz) wholemeal self-raising flour
- 25 g (1 oz) cocoa
- 75 g (3 oz) dried cranberries
- 100 g (approx 4 oz) bar white chocolate, chopped
- 100 g (approx 4 oz) bar milk chocolate, chopped
- 12 pecan halves

1 Put the butter and sugar together in a bowl and mix together with a wooden spoon until soft and fluffy. Gradually beat in the eggs and vanilla extract.

2 Sift in the flour and cocoa and add the cranberries and chocolate. Mix the dough together with your hands. Knead lightly, then wrap in cling film and chill for at least 30 mins.

3 Preheat the oven to 180°C, 350°F or Gas Mark 4. Cover 2 baking sheets with baking parchment. Roll the mixture into 12 balls, arrange well spaced apart on the parchment paper. Flatten each one with the heel of your hand and top each one with a pecan half.

4 Bake for 15 mins until just firm. Leave on the tray for 5 mins to firm up slightly and serve while warm. Or cool on a cooling rack, then store in an airtight container.

Recipe courtesy Billington's and Allinson

We remember when...

Intrepid explorer Sir Edmund Hillary battled his way through strong winds and snow to arrive at the South Pole on January 4, 1958. He was the first explorer to reach the South Pole overland since Captain Scott in 1912. Strangely, on exactly the same day in 2000, the first British women to walk to the South Pole arrived at their destination.

A Grand Day Out

This photograph is of me in March 1954 on Blackpool sands. It was the 'in' thing to have a Montague Burton overcoat with wide lapels, and a trilby hat. I'm at the front with my daughter Sandra, who went on to develop a chain of ladies fashion shops, so fashion runs in the family! **Chris Fawcett, Colne, Lancs**

Chris and his daughter on a chilly day in Blackpool

Superfood!

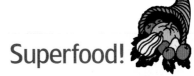

EAT MORE... CARROTS

Packed with...

Calcium, potassium, beta-carotene, fibre, magnesium and phosphorus.

Good for...

Your skin – thought to help reduce wrinkling and protect from sun damage. Also good for maintaining healthy vision and may even help reduce the risk of macular degeneration.

Get more by...

Adding to stews, casseroles and pasta dishes. Also delicious raw – coarsely grate into sandwiches or on to salads. Alternatively, blend up 4 carrots, 2 beets and 2 oranges for a nutritious breakfast drink.

In the kitchen

BEEF STEW AND DUMPLINGS

Serves 4

- 15 ml (1 tablespoon) oil
- 450 g (1 lb) lean beef cubes
- 2 sticks celery, cut into chunks
- 6 baby carrots, peeled and left whole
- ½ small swede
- 2 parsnips, peeled and cut into chunks
- 600 ml (approx 1 pint) English beer or stock
- 15 ml (1 tablespoon) Worcestershire sauce
- 30 ml (2 tablespoons) gravy granules

For the dumplings
- 100g (approx 4oz) self-raising flour
- 50g (2oz) suet
- 15ml (1 tablespoon) wholegrain mustard

1 Heat oil in a pan and cook beef cubes for 4-5 minutes until browned. Transfer to an ovenproof casserole dish. Add the celery, baby carrots, swede and parsnips.

2 Pour over the beer or stock and Worcestershire sauce. Cover and place in preheated oven, 170°C, 325°F, Gas Mark 3, for approximately 2 hours, until the beef is tender.

For the dumplings

3 Mix together the self-raising flour, suet, wholegrain mustard and 75ml (5 tablespoons) water in a bowl, to form a smooth dough. Divide into 8 balls.

4 20 minutes before the end of cooking time, thicken the casserole with the gravy granules and place the dumplings on top. Cook uncovered for remaining cooking time.

Recipe courtesy English Beef & Lamb Executive

Superfood!

EAT MORE... FLAXSEEDS (LINSEEDS)

Packed with...

Iron, manganese, omega-3, 6 and 9 fatty acids, plant fibre, vitamins B3 and E, and phytoestrogen lignin.

Good for...

Improving brain function and helping to prevent osteoporosis, asthma and diabetes. Also thought to help protect the heart by lowering cholesterol.

Get more by...

Blending into your fruit smoothies or sprinkling on to cereals and salads.

We remember when...

The Open University awarded its first degrees on January 11, 1973. Studying for a degree at home opened up avenues for those who hadn't had the opportunity to go to university, and for mature students. It's now the biggest university in the country and computer technology means The Open University has students based all over the world. For more information, log on to www.open.ac.uk or tel: 0845 300 60 90.

AROUND THE HOUSE
Your fridge is the single appliance that uses most energy, and it works more efficiently when it's just full enough to let the air circulation flow freely. So keep it around three quarters full for maximum efficiency.

My childhood home

I grew up in Sheffield in the 1950s. Our house was the centre one of three in a yard, with the toilets at the top end.

At night I made my Dad stand outside the door and whistle so that I knew he was there. In winter we used to put a shovel of hot ash from the fire under the toilet to stop it from freezing.

My tortoise used to hibernate in the toilet, in a straw-filled box, and sometimes she would move about in the straw and scare any visitors who didn't know she was there.

**Pat Holmes,
Grantham,Lincs**

Left: Pat in front of her house, aged four in 1955

A Grand Day Out

During the Second World War and the London Blitz I was one of a small number of choristers remaining in London. I was invited to join the St Paul's and Westminster Abbey Special Choir, which performed at both places of worship.

One day my choirmaster told me I'd been invited to lead the choir at St Paul's Cathedral in the presence of the Royal Family.

On the day, my choirmaster and I travelled to St Paul's, stopping in Leicester Square for lunch. I'd never been in a restaurant before and, with the limited war menu, I think I chose a baked potato.

On the next table were a couple of American Army officers and we all got chatting. When they heard about the reason for our trip, they were most impressed, and before we left, gave me all the chewing gum and candies they had.

The service was wonderful and I wore a red cassock, white surplice and white frilled collar, and two medals from the Royal

Gordon, aged seven (right) and Victor

School of Church Music; and the head chorister's chain, as worn by my brother Victor in the photograph.

To add to my wonderful day, I was taken to the top of St Paul's and saw the views of devastation.

My day continued with a visit to the Lord Mayor of London for tea at the Mansion House. His wife and other dignitaries asked us to sing for them. I finished by singing O For The Wings Of A Dove. I was a very tired but happy boy who had a lot to tell his Mum and Dad.

Gordon Carter, York, N Yorks

Great gardening
Witch hazel

Witch hazels are a delightful shrub in early spring, with bare branches covered in vibrantly coloured flowers. On warm days the scent is intoxicating. Originating in North America and Asia, hamamelis are undemanding plants that thrive in a sunny position in well-drained, slightly acidic soils. The common species Hamamelis mollis has been used to breed a new race of hybrids. One of the newest is H x intermedia 'Robert' which has flowers of deep golden-yellow, edging towards pale orange. Visit www. witchhazelnurseries.co.uk

We remember when...

John F Kennedy was sworn in as president of the United States on January 20, 1961. He was the youngest ever president and his belief in human rights and freedom brought hope to many that a new, peaceful era of world history was beginning. But Kennedy served less than three years before being assassinated in Dallas, Texas.

A Grand Day Out

Dorothy taking a well-earned break

This was an early introduction to my love of the outdoors – rambling, hiking and landscape photography. My Mum and Dad met through a rambling club in the early 1930s, they married and had me, my brother and sister.

I was the eldest and when I was about 12 years old, my parents took the three of us to Holymoorside in Derbyshire.

We travelled by bus to Chesterfield from our nearby village, where Mum bought some fresh rolls and ham – a real treat. We then caught another bus to the country; how I remember sitting on a grassy bank eating our picnic in this wonderful countryside. We'd walked a few miles and I knew at that moment that this was what I wanted to do when I grew up. It only seems like yesterday, so vivid the memory.

Dorothy A Lightfoot, Keyworth, Notts

In the kitchen

■ LEMON AND SULTANA CURD TARTS ■
Makes 8

- ■ 500 g (approx 1 ¼ lb) pack shortcrust pastry
- ■ 4 large eggs
- ■ 450 g (1 lb) tub curd cheese
- ■ 100 g (approx 4 oz) caster sugar
- ■ Zest and juice of 2 lemons
- ■ 75 g (3 oz) sultanas

To decorate
- ■ Icing sugar, to dust

1 Preheat the oven to 200°C, 400°F or Gas Mark 6.
2 Roll out the pastry and use to line 8 individual fluted flan tins which measure 8cm (3 ¼ inch) across the base. Prick the bases with a fork and place on a metal baking sheet.
3 Beat the eggs, cheese and sugar together, and stir in the lemon zest, juice and sultanas. Divide the mixture between the pastry cases.
4 Bake for 25-30 minutes or until just set and pale golden on top. Leave to cool in the tins.
5 Carefully remove from the tins and serve dusted with icing sugar.
■ Tip: You can also cook this mixture in a 20cm (8 inch) fluted flan tin. Add an extra 15-20 minutes to the baking time.

Recipe courtesy Lion Quality Eggs

TOP TIP

Add a couple of squirts of lemon juice to rice pudding. This helps keep the rice lovely and white, and stops it from sticking.

Maureen Thayre, Kirriemuir, Angus

Great gardening
Annual climbers

O ne of the best ways of creating impact in your garden is with annual climbers - these put on several metres of growth in just one season and are covered in flowers all summer. Always popular is 'Morning Glory', ipomoea, and the newest variety on the market is definitely worth a try. 'Candy Pink', which is exclusive to Thompson and Morgan, is spectacular, producing large, pastel pink blooms with a distinct paler cross along the centre. Sow the seeds now and, when the young plants are large enough, plant three at the base of a piece of trellis, a pergola or obelisk and enjoy.

■ You can order seed, tel: 01473 688 821 or visit www.thompson-morgan.com

Superfood!
EAT MORE... TURNIPS

Packed with...

Vitamins C, A and K, potassium, folic acid, phosphorus, calcium and magnesium.

Good for...

Clearing the blood of toxins, purifying the body, cleaning teeth, aiding digestion and protecting against certain cancers.

Get more by...

Thinly slicing to accompany a spicy dip, serving cubed in a rich meaty stew or mashing with potatoes for a tangy mash with a difference.

■ AROUND THE HOUSE ■

Don't store medicines in the bathroom as heat and a steamy atmosphere can affect their potency. Keep them in a dry, cool place on high shelves in cupboards.

My childhood home

I grew up in the middle one of three grooms' cottages (circa 19th century) during the Second World War. Although it looked like a bungalow, there were two bedrooms in the attic, one of which was over the living room of the house next door.

My sister and I were playing in our attic bedroom one morning and we discovered a hinge behind the papered wall. Further investigation revealed a little door! We couldn't wait to tell our friends and decided to see what treasures lay behind the door at the first opportunity.

Parents at the cinema, four of us set off on an adventure. My sister went first, stepping on the wooden rafters. One friend

Elizabeth's childhood home

followed, missed her footing and disappeared through the gap, landing on the living room floor of the house next door!

Fortunately, for us, they were out and Eileen wasted no time in picking herself up and making a quick exit through the front door. Both friends scurried home as fast

as they could, leaving us to face the music.

Mum and Dad guessed what had happened the moment the irate neighbours showed them the ceiling. It was fortunate for us that they were related to the landlady and had the repair done for free.

Elizabeth Stevens, Derby

My childhood home

Gwen on a sunnier day in the 1940s

The deep snow of 1947 failed to dampen our joy when my family moved into a prefab. What delight to have a fridge, a washer and more cupboards than we ever dreamed of.

I was six at the time and to me it was a palace. But imagine my horror when, two weeks later, Mum lost her keys. Locked out in snowdrifts, we hailed the builders who were still on site erecting the prefabs.

"Okay," yelled a young Scottish fellow, "we'll soon get you back in, but we'll have to use a tin opener to open up the roof!" My heart sank and I began to cry. Luckily our new friend provided a spare key and my tears were soon wiped away.

We lived happily in our 'tin home' for 15 years – hot in summer, cold in winter.

Gwen Spain, Gloucester

TOP TIP

A thick slice of bread is excellent for wiping up broken glass. It takes up the splinters more safely than tissue.

Mrs Aldridge, Baldock, Herts

Great gardening

Snowdrops

The pure white, nodding, bell-like flowers of snowdrops charm even non-gardeners, so they should be planted in every garden. Natives of Europe, Iran and Turkey, there are many different species and naturally selected cultivars to choose between and one of the most recent is 'Colossus', which has really large blooms. One of the best places to see snowdrops is at the Cambo Estate in Scotland where the gardens look magical during February, because the snowdrops have naturalised so extensively they look like snow!

You can order snowdrops during spring while they're 'in the green' by calling 01333 450 054 or visiting www.camboestate.com

Superfood!

EAT MORE... LEEKS

Packed with...

Vitamins A and K, calcium, folic acid and potassium.

Good for...

Cleansing the body and relieving the symptoms of gout.

Get more by...

Stir-frying with a handful of sesame seeds or baking with a creamy cheese sauce and topping with breadcrumbs.

In the kitchen

PORK TORTILLA WRAPS

Serves 4

- 450 g (1 lb) lean pork fillet
- 10 ml (2 teaspoons) fajita seasoning
- 50 g (2 oz) mushrooms, sliced
- 1 carrot, peeled and grated
- 1/2 courgette, finely chopped
- 1/2 red pepper, finely chopped
- 6-8 flour tortilla wraps

For the salsa

- 2 tomatoes, chopped
- 1 x 200 g (7 oz) can sweetcorn, drained
- 1/2 red pepper, deseeded and sliced
- 1/2 courgette, peeled and grated
- Juice of 1/2 lime
- 30 ml (2 tablespoons) fresh coriander, chopped
- 15 ml (1 tablespoon) olive oil

1. To make the salsa, mix together the tomatoes, sweetcorn, red pepper, courgette, lime juice, coriander and olive oil.
2. Cut the pork fillet into thin slices and dry fry in a hot, non-stick wok for 5-6 minutes. Add the fajita seasoning and mushrooms, carrot, courgette and red pepper, and cook for a further 1-2 minutes.
3. Serve the pork piled into wraps with salsa, dips and crunchy salad leaves.

Recipe courtesy Love Pork

A Grand Day Out

I had many favourite Sundays out, all to Barley in Hertfordshire. This little village is where I spent four years of my childhood with the most wonderful foster parents, who my sister and I called Grandma and Granddad Jackson, and their daughter, Auntie Glad. They opened their home and hearts to two London evacuees and we were happy and contented, but our own parents thought we were growing away from them, so we came home before the end of the war.

We didn't forget them but returned often, and when my sister and I took an interest in cycling in our mid teens, our Sundays were a joy.

We cycled the 30 miles from London to Barley, as there were few cars. We would stop at Ware for a rest, and bathe our feet in the River Lea until one day an official came along and asked: "Do you realise you're washing your feet in London's water supply?"

I've visited Barley every year since we left, and my friends have been given a guided tour!

Margaret Norgan, Harlow, Essex

Above: Auntie Glad and Grandma Jackson with Margaret (front left), her sister Jean and a friend

We remember when...

Elvis knocked Johnny Tillotson's Poetry in Motion from the number one spot on January 26, 1961, with his ballad Are You Lonesome Tonight - the perfect song for all those Saturday Night dances! Elvis went on to have three more number ones that year, with Wooden Heart (March), Surrender (June) and His Latest Flame (November).

AROUND THE HOUSE

You've just had the living room carpeted and someone spills red wine on it. Whatever you do, don't sprinkle salt on it. Salt will stop the stain spreading but you'll never get rid of the residue. Better to blot (not rub) it with paper towels, working from the outside in, dilute it with water, then blot again.

We remember when...

The space race took on a new dimension this week in 1961 when America sent a chimpanzee, named Ham, into space in a rocket as an experiment to see if a human might survive in space. Ham was found alive and well on January 31 near Cape Canaveral, around 400 miles from the launch pad. Apparently he'd suffered no ill effects from the experience.

A Grand Day Out

In the early 1970s I organised a Cultural Society in the school where I worked. Parents were involved and regularly joined the girls on the outings. One Saturday we visited Canterbury and it was on this day that my future husband, Bob, and I got to know each other as we visited the city's sights.

After this, we visited many interesting places and our annual visit to Spalding's Tulip Parade was a highlight. The floats were grand, the displays skilfully created, and such a great atmosphere in the sunshine.

After the parade, we'd go back to the coach for a tulip field tour, then to a village hall for tea, and afterwards a visit to a beautifully decorated church - a day of such splendid colour!

Priscilla Odell, Hampton, Middx

A beautiful colourful tulip float

In the kitchen

▮ RAISIN AND CINNAMON EGGY BREAD ▮

Serves 4

- ▮ A little oil for frying
- ▮ 4 large eggs
- ▮ 6 slices raisin and cinnamon loaf
- ▮ Blueberries, raspberries and crème fraîche to serve

1 Heat a little oil in a non-stick frying pan. Beat the eggs in a shallow dish. Dip the slices of raisin bread in the egg, turning until coated, then add to the hot pan.
2 Cook 2-3 slices at a time, for 4-5 minutes, turning over once until they are golden on both sides. Transfer to a plate and keep warm. Repeat with the remaining egg and bread.
3 To serve, cut the eggy bread slices in half and arrange three pieces per person. Scatter over a few blueberries and raspberries, and serve with crème fraîche.

Recipe courtesy Lion Quality Eggs

▮ AROUND THE HOUSE ▮

Try this as a window cleaner: 1 part white vinegar to 1 part water, plus a few drops of liquid soap. To make it easier to see streaks when cleaning windows, use side-to-side strokes on one side and up-and-down strokes on the other. Buff to a shine with crumpled newspaper.

▮ TOP TIP ▮

Rub a little petroleum jelly inside the top and on the grooves of a bottle of nail varnish for easy opening.

Mrs A Chambers, London W6

Great gardening
Narcissus

You know spring has arrived when the yellow buds of narcissi start to ripen. Plant breeders are racing ahead in their attempts to find a pink variety and one of the newest on the market is 'Dreamcatcher' which was bred by Eddie Jarman. Raised by crossing 'China Doll' with 'Culmination' in 1993, the resultant seedling first flowered in 1998. It's only now, after nine years of trials that it has been catalogued. With a peach-coloured trumpet and pale yellow outer petals, it'll be a real talking point.

■ You can order it from Ringhaddy Daffodils by calling 0289 7541007. More readily available is 'Pink Parasol' which produces magnificent pink-frilled cups and white petals. It's available from Van Meuwen, tel 0870 241 1850 or visit www.vanmeuwen.co.uk

Superfood!

EAT MORE... PARSNIPS

Packed with...

Folic acid, magnesium, calcium, potassium and phosphorus.

Good for...

Cleansing and detoxifying the body and helping the kidneys and spleen. Also thought to help keep the bowels regular.

Get more by...

Thinly slicing and baking in olive oil along with strips of carrot – the perfect homemade healthy crisp!

My childhood home

My childhood home was a three-storey house in Paddington - Portnal Road. Mum, Dad, my older brother and younger sister and I lived in three rooms on the ground floor. There was no bathroom or inside toilet, though the people upstairs had one each.

The front door knocker was shared, one knock for us; two and three for those upstairs.

Above us lived a widow, and above her an elderly couple. I can see them now, going up the stairs in the darkness, and when they got to the top, I could see the old lady's pink bloomers over her knees as she got to the first landing. I always giggled at that.

The walls were damp, so Dad had to decorate often, as the wallpaper got stained by the wet, and the electric sockets were green where the damp came through.

The coalman carried his sacks to the cupboard under the stairs, and you could hear the coal dust under his feet as he trod on the lino. When we

Above: Two-year-old Doris outside her front door, in 1948
Left: Doris on leave from the WRAC in 1966

had to get a shovel of coal for the fire, I was pretty sharpish as you could often hear a mouse scuffling about. I often dropped the shovel and ran to mum.

It was no palace, but we were happy enough!

Doris Pick, Slough

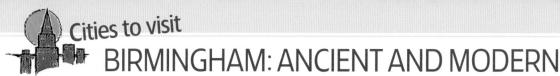

BIRMINGHAM: ANCIENT AND MODERN

Hancock's home town

Manufacturing has been important in Birmingham for centuries and many of its modern attractions pay tribute to its past industrial might. Vehicle production was long associated with the Midlands and some vintage examples can be seen at the Aston Road Transport Museum, formerly Witton tram depot.

More romantically, craft and jewellery have played an important role in the city's history of manufacturing. The jewellery quarter discovery centre is housed in the workshops of a family firm called Smith & Pepper whose former employees helped to restore the museum to its original state.

For youngsters, one of the city's hidden gems is the Nature Centre in Edgbaston that is home to more than 130 species of animals. The six-acre site also contains the Lilliput Village.

Visitors to Birmingham can enjoy a range of domestic architecture from the grand to the most humble. Aston Hall, a Jacobean country house, was built for the influential Holte family. At the other end

of the social scale, back-to-back terraced houses have been preserved by the National Trust in a courtyard near the Hippodrome in Hurst Street.

The Pre-Raphaelite artist Edward Burne-Jones was born in Birmingham in 1833 and St Philip's Cathedral has stained glasses designed by him.

In Old Square, a remarkable statue pays homage to one of Birmingham's best-loved sons, comedian Tony Hancock who was born at 41 Southam Road. Unveiled by Sir Harry Secombe in 1996, the affectionate tribute depicts Hancock in his trademark Homburg hat enjoying a nice cup of tea.

Hot Horlicks and calk

Marian Cunliffe of Pudsey roamed free in rural Cumbria

Our village

On a breezy, sunlit day my family arrived to live in the village of Hayton, near Carlisle. We lived in one of two cottages belonging to the beautiful old house called Westgarth, where my father worked.

Nearby was the village smithy where all day could be heard the clatter of horses' hooves as they came to be shod.

I made friends with two sisters from a farm. Together we went for walks and picnics with their collie dog, Merry. We built ourselves a somewhat draughty log cabin.

We discovered some glorious walks. Not far away the River Gelt had carved its way through moss-covered boulders amid woodland of ferny hollows and dappled shade. Another favourite walk was to a hamlet known as Hayton Townhead. Here the woodland was of tall pines rising darkly above the houses. A cobbled track rose steadily upwards to a boulder known as the Greystone from where there were views for miles around with the silvery ribbon of the Solway Firth gleaming in the distance.

I attended the Church of England school. It was a long, low

building of mellowed stone. A bell in a small belfry hung above the door. Inside were bare boards and the smell of ink, chalk and books.

The school was efficiently heated by a vast iron monster of a stove. Every time the lid was lifted for refuelling it roared like a furnace and the sparks flew upwards. It was most comforting on icy mornings when we clustered around it, waiting for lessons to begin.

For the payment of a halfpenny you could purchase a small beaker of steaming Horlicks dispensed by the headmaster from a small metal urn.

Quiz of the decade

PIC: REX FEATURES

Fab Forties

1 What age was Winston Churchill when he became prime minister in 1940?
A 60
B 55
C 61
D 65

2 The first post-war Winter Olympic Games were held in?
A Oslo, Norway
B St Moritz, Switzerland
C Montreal, Canada
D Amsterdam, Holland

3 The Polaroid Camera was invented in 1947 by?
A Edward Hand
B Edwin Land
C Richard Landing
D Benjamin Spock

4 Humphrey Bogart (pictured) achieved his first 'top line billing' in the classic 1941 film noir, The Maltese Falcon. The role had previously been turned down by?
A Edward G. Robinson
B James Cagney
C Paul Henreid
D George Raft

5 In 1942 Frank Sinatra had his first hit as a solo performer with a song penned by Cole Porter. But which was it?
A Night And Day
B I Get A Kick Out Of You
C I Love Paris
D All Through The Night

6 Which classic novel by George Orwell was first published in 1949?
A Animal Farm
B Coming Up For Air
C Burmese Days
D 1984

7 French engineer Louis Reard invented the bikini in?
A 1940
B 1946
C 1949
D 1947

8 In July 1942 the UK ration per person for chocolate and sweets was set at?
A 2oz
B 4oz
C 1oz
D 5oz

9 China became a Communist nation in?
A 1945
B 1946
C 1941
D 1949

10 Who won the 1947 FA Cup?
A Liverpool
B Charlton Athletic
C Manchester City
D Burnley

Answers: 1D, 2B, 3B, 4D, 5A, 6D, 7B, 8A, 9D, 10B

THE FULL PICTURE

BY PETER CAUNT

Jigsaws prove a lifesaver for recently widowed Brian

"You need to get out more, Dad."

Brian looked across at Barbara. She looked heartbreakingly like her mother; the same blue eyes, the same smile.

"It's been over a year since Mum died. She wouldn't have wanted you to grieve for the rest of your life."

"I do go out. I'm here having lunch with you and Amy." He leaned across and grasped his granddaughter's tiny hand.

"You know what I mean, Dad."

Brian did know what she meant. For weeks after the funeral he had not left the house. He didn't like meeting people, dreading their awkward sympathy and well-meant offers of help. His wife's death had been so sudden – just when they were planning their retirement years.

He shook himself, and turned to smile at dimple-cheeked Amy. Their lunches together had kept Brian going through the dreary winter months.

"Is that another jigsaw from the charity shop?" Barbara said, looking at the battered box by her father's chair. "I know it takes your mind off things, but you do need to mix more with people, Dad."

She knew the empty family house was full of memories. And it had been even lonelier for him since she and David had moved

away. At least she and Amy could visit him regularly but she always had to rush back to meet the older children from school.

"I've found a charity shop where the helpers are new around here. Makes it easier, no need to chat. And they have a good selection of secondhand jigsaws."

"Is that where you bought that one?" she inquired, pointing at the box.

"Yes, but I'm going to take it back. There's a piece missing. It's happened a few times before and they are very good about exchanging them."

'We're running a charity shop not a dating agency'

"Well, we need to be getting back. I'll ring you later and we'll be over as usual next week. Are you sure you're okay?"

"Don't worry about me. You just take good care of my granddaughter."

Picking Amy up, Brian gave her a kiss and strapped her into her pushchair. Barbara hugged him: "Bye, Dad."

Brian watched them until they disappeared around the corner to the car park, then he set off down the high street, head bowed against the February drizzle,

hoping not to bump into anyone he knew.

He made a pretence of examining the display in the charity shop window – he could see there were a couple of customers inside. He was in no particular hurry and slowly took in the array of old videos, scented candles and dog-eared paperbacks. The door opened and the two customers left. Brian entered.

The same two volunteers were there. Eleanor was tall and thin and her name badge was pinned to her tweed jacket with military precision. Her manner was brusque. Janet could not have been more different. Small and plumpish, she wore brightly-patterned dresses and often forgot to put on her name badge. Brian could imagine her back in the swinging Sixties, wearing flowers in her hair.

To his disappointment, Eleanor was stationed behind the counter while Janet had disappeared into the back to sort through donated goods. Eleanor regarded him severely through her glasses.

"I bought this jigsaw last week," he stammered, "but there seems to be a piece missing."

"This is the third one you've brought back!"

"I'm sorry, but you did say that if there was any problem I could return it."

He put the last piece in place and sat back in his chair

Tim Sharville.©om

"I suppose you want a replacement," Eleanor grumbled.

"If it's not too much trouble."

Sighing, she took the box from him and went into the storeroom.

Brian browsed through the rail of men's shirts, trying to position himself so that he could see into the storeroom.

"Another returned jigsaw from Mr Brown."

"Oh," said Janet, "shall I deal with it?"

Eleanor gave her the same stare she had bestowed on Brian. "You sold him the last two, didn't you?"

Janet gazed at the floor, but didn't reply.

"I'm sure all the jigsaws were complete: I checked them myself."

"Some of the pieces could have dropped out of the box," suggested Janet helpfully.

Eleanor's stare hardened. "I've seen you looking at him! At your age! Removing pieces from the boxes so he has to come back."

"But he's lonely and doesn't get out much."

Eleanor rolled her eyes heavenwards: "We're running a charity shop, not a dating agency."

Janet blushed.

Eleanor said: "I'm going to give him the jigsaw that came in yesterday. The box was still sealed so I know all the pieces are there."

Brian heard their voices but could not tell what the discussion was about. He quickly turned to examine the bric-a-brac as

Eleanor returned with the new puzzle. Janet appeared at the storeroom door and he gave her an embarrassed smile before leaving.

The following afternoon he started the jigsaw. It was quite an intricate one, a view of the North Yorkshire moors. Gradually, he fitted together all the edge pieces. On the third day, he put the last piece in place and sat back in his chair. Then he took a piece from the centre. Going to the back door, he looked around carefully before deliberately putting the single piece into his dustbin. Then, smiling to himself, he went back inside to make his tea.

Friday

1

....

Saturday

2

....

Sunday

3

....

Monday

4

....

Tuesday

5
Shrove Tuesday

....

Wednesday

6
Ash Wednesday

....

Thursday

7
Chinese New Year (Year of the Rat)

....

Friday

8

....

Saturday

9

....

Sunday

10

....

Monday

11

....

Tuesday

12
Yours magazine on sale

....

Wednesday

13

....

Thursday

14
Valentine's Day

....

Friday

15

....

Saturday

16

....

Sunday

17

....

Monday

18

....

Tuesday

19

....

Wednesday

20

....

Thursday

21

....

Friday

22

....

Saturday **23**	Wednesday **27**
Sunday **24**	Thursday **28**
Monday **25**	Friday **29**
Tuesday **26**	

Yours magazine on sale

PIC: REX FEATURES

Born this month

Sir David Jason (pictured) was born on February 2, 1940 in Edmonton, London. He was born David John White but changed his surname to Jason when he began acting, as there was already a David White on Equity's books – the actors' union.

Married this month

Judi Dench married British actor Michael Williams on February 2 1971. They had a daughter, Tara Cressida Williams, in 1972 who later became an actress. Michael died aged 65, in 2001.

Died this month

Karen Carpenter, of pop band The Carpenters died on February 4, 1983 at the age of 32. She died from heart failure related to the eating condition anorexia nervosa, which she'd been battling since the 1970s.

A Grand Day Out

I try to confine any delusions of grandeur I may have – such as meeting the Queen – to dreams. When my eldest daughter, Pauline, was five the Queen came to open the new M62 motorway between Lancashire and Yorkshire. "I'm going to meet the Queen!" she announced. Off she went on the bus with her classmates to Scammonden to see the Queen cut the ribbon.

Meeting the bus at the school gate at 4 o'clock, I watched while 55 infants clutching Union Jacks leapt out into the scoop of mums and grandmas. There was no sign of Pauline – I had visions of my little lamb being left on the Pennine Moors – but no, there she was, curled up in a ball, sleeping fitfully on the front seat.

"She didn't come in a white dress and she didn't have a crown." A few more sobs, and then: "She didn't have a horse and carriage – just a fast black car and I never saw her."

Three years later a fine cream envelope dropped through our letterbox. It had a royal coat of arms embossed in red and was addressed to Miss Pauline M Walker. Trying to sound casual, I met her from school with: "Oh, by the way, there's a letter for you from Buckingham Palace."

"Oh, I thought the Queen would

Bright-eyed Pauline, aged 7

reply," said Pauline nonchalantly. Royal disappointment number two was obvious, as she read,

Dear Pauline, Her Majesty the Queen has asked me to thank you for your letter asking if you could accompany your grandparents to the Palace Garden Party in July. Unfortunately, their invitation does not extend to other guests. However, I hope they will enjoy the party and will tell you all about it, and that one day you may receive your own personal invitation. Signed, Lady-in-Waiting to HM Queen Elizabeth 11.

Thirty years on and she's still hoping for a meeting. Not such a trifling affair as motorway opening or garden parties. She now dreams of finding the cure for Alzheimer's and being honoured by becoming a Dame. Where does she get such fanciful ideas? I'm sure I don't know, but I'm just off to Llandudno for an Investiture hat, in case mums can go too!

**Margaret Walker,
Porthmadog, Gwynedd**

Great gardening
Hellebore

Specialists in the breeding of hellebores, Ashwood's Nursery near Birmingham, produces great new cultivars with amazing regularity. With hybrids of H orientalis showing the most promise – they produce flowers in a wide range of colours, as well as doubles, singles and anemone-centred types – breeding has now moved on to creating plants which hold their heads more upright so you don't have to bend over to enjoy the blooms.

■ There are always plenty of new cultivars listed on the nursery's website at www.ashwood-nurseries.co.uk. Alternatively, tel: 01384 401 996.

In the kitchen

▩ APHRODISIAC'S CRÈME BRÛLÉE ▩
Serves 2

- ▪ 100 ml (3 ½ fl oz) milk
- ▪ 150 ml (pint) double cream
- ▪ 1 large egg
- ▪ 2 egg yolks
- ▪ Salt and pepper
- ▪ 50 g (2 oz) asparagus tips, cut into 5 cm (2 in) lengths
- ▪ 15 g (approx ½ oz) freshly grated Parmesan cheese

1 Preheat the oven to 170°C, 325°F or Gas Mark 3. Heat the milk and cream together in a small pan until almost boiling. Beat the egg and egg yolks together with seasoning. Pour the hot milk on to the eggs and mix well.

2 Divide the asparagus between four 175 ml (6 fl oz) ramekin dishes, then pour over the egg mixture. Stand the dishes in a roasting tin and pour boiling water from the kettle to come half way up the outside of the dishes. Bake for 25-30 mins or until just set.

3 Meanwhile, line a baking sheet with non-stick baking paper and sprinkle the cheese into four 6-7cm (or 2 ¾ in) rounds. Bake for 6-8 mins until golden brown – the cheese will melt and spread to make lacy wafers. Leave to cool slightly.

4 To serve, remove the brulées from the oven and cool for 5 mins. Serve topped with the parmesan crisps, and toast fingers. Recipe courtesy Lion Quality Eggs

We remember when...

Sweet rationing ending in Britain on February 5, 1953, after more than ten years of shortages. Sugar was still rationed, but it was such a treat to queue for toffee apples, aniseed balls, sherbet fountains and liquorice strips after school! An earlier attempt to de-ration sweets in 1949 had failed as suppliers couldn't keep up with demand!

My childhood home

I lived in a colliery cottage in Cinder Hill, Nottingham, as my father worked for the coal board. It was stone with wooden beams, and the toilet was across the yard. The cottage had one large kitchen and living room downstairs with two bedrooms upstairs.

Dad bred canaries and we had one called Jimmy who sang so sweetly you could hear him at the top of the yard. Dad had an allotment, and I used to take Peter, the dog, and the radio and sit listening to it in the deckchair. I had a great childhood.

Ann Rowlatt, Deeping St James, Lincs
Right: Ann in the garden with Peter
Below: Ann in front of her house

Superfood!
▩ EAT MORE... CABBAGE

Packed with...

Vitamins C, E and K, magnesium, phosphorus, chlorophyll, iron, potassium and iodine.

Good for...

Reducing stress and preventing heart disease and anaemia. Also thought to aid digestion and soothe stomach inflammation.

Get more by...

Stir-frying with baby sweetcorn and strips of carrot or blending up a stomach-soothing smoothie, adding chunks of pineapple and fresh ginger.

In the kitchen

CUPID'S CALFOUTIS

Serves 6

- Oil for greasing
- 450 g (1 lb) fresh cherries, pitted or 400 g (14 oz) can pitted black cherries, drained
- 60 ml (4 tablespoons) kirsch or cherry brandy
- 100 ml (4 fl oz) milk
- 150 ml ($^1/_4$ pint) whipping cream
- $^1/_2$ teaspoon vanilla essence
- 4 large eggs
- 100 g (approx 3 $^1/_2$ oz) caster sugar
- 25 g (1 oz) plain flour

To decorate
- Icing sugar, to dust
- Whipped cream, to serve

1 Preheat the oven to 200°C, 400°F or Gas Mark 6. Lightly oil a 23 cm (9 in) wide ovenproof dish. Mix the cherries and kirsch or brandy together and set aside.

2 Put the milk, cream and vanilla essence in a pan and heat until almost boiling. In a large bowl, beat the eggs and sugar until creamy, add the flour and beat until smooth. Pour over the hot milk and mix well. You can leave the mixture to stand for up to 1 hour.

3 Scatter the cherries over the base of the dish. Stir the batter, and pour over the cherries. Bake for 30-35 minutes or until risen and puffy. Dust with icing sugar and serve warm or cold with whipped cream.

Recipe courtesy Lion Quality Eggs

TOP TIP

Save pieces of old net curtain and cut to the size required, fold in half and sew along two edges to make a bag to wash your delicates in. Tie a length of wool round the top to fasten securely.

D Sibley, Billericay, Essex

Superfood!

EAT MORE... OYSTERS

Packed with...

Iron, vitamins A, C and B12 and zinc.

Good for...

Sexual health, as well as the immune system and helping to maintain a healthy cardiovascular system.

Get more by...

Steaming with finely chopped fresh ginger and garlic or serving raw in their shells to your loved one on Valentine's Day.

We remember when...

Our favourite figure-skating couple Jayne Torvill and Christopher Dean won the gold medal at the Winter Olympics in Sarajevo, in the former Yugoslavia, on February 14, 1984. The winning couple skated to the seductive beats of Ravel's Bolero, an appropriate choice for Valentine's Day! That year, both were awarded BBC Sports Personality Of The Year and a year later, the OBE.

AROUND THE HOUSE

Here's an easy way to patch wallpaper up (providing you've some left over from decorating). Tear (don't cut) a piece of wallpaper slightly larger than the damaged area but roughly the same shape. Glue the back and stick down over the damaged part. Match the pattern and use a mini-roller to flatten the edges.

My childhood home

Although I don't remember much about the house I was born in, one thing is very clear. We had a small room between the kitchen and the toilet which was used for storing coal.

When the sirens went in the war, we would shelter in this cupboard and it always amuses me to remember that one brick was missing on the wall between ours and next door's house.

If we wanted to talk to the neighbour, we'd knock on the wall with a hammer and talk to each other through the hole. It all seemed quite normal at the time!

Christine Jay, Southampton

Left: Christine, aged 5, outside her house in 1942

A Grand Day Out

My favourite day out was the day I spent with my Aunt Emma who was manageress of the Victoria Wine Company, King's Road, Chelsea. I was eight years old and went to my aunt's by bus, which was a treat in itself.

It was raining and downstairs was full, so we had to go upstairs. Buses were open top in the 1920s and a piece of waterproof sheeting was attached to the back of each seat, which you put over your knees, an umbrella protecting the rest of you.

The morning was spent helping auntie in the shop. Bottles were wrapped in brown paper, which auntie showed me how to do; and to hand out the correct change – I felt so important.

It was early closing day, and we went for afternoon tea with a titled lady auntie had become friendly with who was a customer.

A maid answered the door and showed us into the drawing room. I'd been told not to speak unless I was spoken to. Lady E

Rita with Aunt Emma

rang a little bell and the maid appeared with a silver tea service and a plate of fancy iced-cakes – mouthwatering, as we only ever had rock cakes at home.

After tea, Lady E asked me if I would like to see her daughter's playroom; the maid appeared and escorted me up to this wonderland. The daughter was called Raine and was away at boarding school. There was the most wonderful doll's house I'd ever seen, and a row of dolls along the bed. The maid asked me if I would like to hold one but told me not to tell Madam.

When I left I remembered auntie's instructions and said: "Thank you for having me."

Rita Woodley, Tonbridge, Kent

Great gardening

Beaujolais Bonnets

If you choose carefully, you'll find that many herbaceous perennials will flower in their first year if sown early enough. One of the most popular cottage garden plants is scabious, and Thompson and Morgan released a new variety recently called 'Beaujolais Bonnets' which will flower this summer if sown now. The plants are bushy and are covered with burgundy flowers that boast pale outer petals and white stamens – a wonderful combination. It's a great choice if you want to attract butterflies into the garden.

■ Tel: 01473 688 821 or visit www.thompson-morgan.com

We remember when...

Popstars Lulu and Maurice Gibb, of the Bee Gees tried to marry in secret in a Buckinghamshire church on February 8, 1969. But the thousands of screaming fans at the church meant police had to help the couple through the crowd. The next month, Lulu represented the UK in the Eurovision Song Contest which she won with her song, Boom Bang-a-Bang.

A Grand Day Out

I was an only child but my grandmother was a registered foster mother and her house was always full of children. So on days out, Mum, Dad, Gran and I – plus the children (including babies) piled into Dad's car and he'd head to Southend or Margate.

Southend was the best because of the shop near the pier where they cooked sausage, mash and onions in the window. My friend, Avril, and I used to lean on the window for as long as possible. Then on with the rubber shoes to brave the mud before the tide caught us. We had some lovely times.

Molly Barnett, Grays, Essex

Molly, her mum (both extreme left) and Gran on a day out in the 1930s

TOP TIP

Keep a magnifying glass in the kitchen to read the small print on instructions, or to read a list of ingredients. **Mrs Rae Ward, Bedford**

In the kitchen

BRISKET IN CIDER
Serves 4 – 6

- ■ 15 ml (1 tablespoon) oil
- ■ 1.25 kg (2 ½ lb) lean beef brisket joint
- ■ 2 onions, quartered
- ■ 3 eating apples, cut in half
- ■ 1 cinnamon stick
- ■ 5 ml (1 teaspoon) ground ginger
- ■ 150 ml (¼ pint) cider

For Apple & Rhubarb Chutney
- ■ 2 sticks rhubarb, cut into chunks
- ■ 1 eating apple, cored and sliced
- ■ 2 large pinches ground ginger
- ■ 60 ml (4 tablespoons) cider
- ■ 45 ml (3 tablespoons) mead
- ■ ½ cinnamon stick

1 Heat the oil in a large, lidded casserole dish and brown a lean beef brisket joint on all sides. Add the onions, apples, cinnamon stick and ground ginger to the pan.
2 Pour over the cider, cover and simmer on hob or in the oven at 170°C, 325°F or Gas Mark 3 for 30-40 minutes per 1 lb/1/2kg, plus 30-40 minutes extra.
3 Either serve hot or allow to cool in the cider; transfer to a cold pan or bowl to cool down quicker.
4 For the chutney, place the rhubarb, apple, ground ginger, cider, mead (if mead is not available, use all cider or apple juice) and the ½ cinnamon stick into a pan. Cook over a gentle heat for 5-10 minutes until softened. Add a little sugar to taste if necessary.
5 Serve thinly sliced with salad or in sandwiches with the apple and rhubarb chutney. Alternatively serve hot with potatoes and seasonal vegetables, using the sauce as a thin gravy.

Recipe courtesy English Beef & Lamb Executive

Great gardening

Marigolds

Marigolds are often looked down on as being common, but they're so colourful and long-lasting that they deserve a place in every garden. The wild relative may be indiginous but it's the highly bred cousins which add welcome splashes of colour. Calendula 'Princess Orange and Black' produces a blaze of orange flowers during the summer – its fiery petals contrasting well with the almost black centre. Scorching in colour, the blooms have beautifully quilled petals and are produced on long stems which makes them ideal for cutting.

■ A new variety from Mr Fothergill's Seeds, you can order seeds, tel: 0845 1662511 or www.mr-fothergills.com

Superfood!

▧ EAT MORE... GRAPEFRUIT ▧

Packed with...

Vitamin C, magnesium, potassium and calcium.

Good for...

Relieving arthritic symptoms, cleansing the blood, maintaining a healthy cardiovascular system and preventing throat infections.

Get more by...

Using to top sorbets, ice-cream and cheesecake or making a citrus chicken dish – squeeze the juice over a chicken before placing the grapefruit halves inside the cavity, seasoning with garlic powder and roasting.

▧ AROUND THE HOUSE ▧

Make your bedroom a place of peace and calm by keeping clutter to a minimum, and if you have trouble sleeping, clear your mind by writing down what's on your mind, then resolve to tackle it in the morning.

My childhood home

Myra outside her house, aged 13 in 1948

Emotions flood back to me – even at 72 - when I remember the house where I was born, an end-of-terrace with three bedrooms, no bathroom and an outside toilet. I was born in the front room on a cold, snowy February, Father traipsing the streets in the snow to fetch the midwife.

Although it was an ordinary house in an ordinary road, my Mother worked hard to keep it clean and as I grew older, was expected to help with the jobs.

It was during the war that I came to appreciate my home. After a claustrophobic night in the shelter, to come out into the fresh air – often after a night of bombing – to see our house still standing was a such a welcome sight.

My house was a place I could invite my friends for a cup of cocoa and some dripping toast after school on wintry days. The place where I had my birthday parties – when the pale blue bone china set with camels around the rims, which my uncle had brought back from Egypt after the war – came out of safe-keeping for the occasion.

Our house had an added bonus – we lived at the top of a hill that led down to Walthamstow Avenue Football Club grounds, sadly no more.

The house was eventually sold and I think the folk that bought it still own it. I hope they, too, will be left with many happy memories of the house where I was born.

Myra Barklem, London E4

My childhood home

Our house was built in the 1930s, but had a bathroom and an indoor toilet, as Dad worked for Percy Bilton the builders. This was in North London. Dad created a large garden from a blank space – including a vegetable garden - and we also kept chickens which I used to feed. So we were able to help the neighbours out with eggs and vegs.

During the war when the buzz bombs were dropped over London, Mum and I used to creep under the stairs, taking pillows, a torch and some books, and I used to have a lovely time. Dad was in the ARP, so would be out in the evenings, checking on people's windows in the blackout.

I lived there for about 30 years before moving into my own home. I'll never forget the years I spent at home with my parents, it prepared me for life in the only way a real home can.

**Hazel Malt,
Broadstairs, Kent**

Great gardening

Monardas

Great in herbacous borders, medicinally and as a herb, monardas more than earn a place in the garden. Although natives of North America, these plants haves wormed their way into our affections. One of the newest cultivars, 'Bergamo', won a Fleuroselect Gold Medal (an international organisation for the ornamental plants industry). It flowers early in the season, produces magnificent whorls of purple flowers right up the plant and, being an annual, can be sown each spring – reducing the risk of it spreading invasively. At only 65cm in height, it's shorter than most perennial varieties, making it ideal in a smaller garden.

■ Seeds are available from Plants of Distinction and can be ordered, tel: 0870 4609445 or www.plantsofdistinction.co.uk

AROUND THE HOUSE

For all those knitters, crocheters and tapestry fans out there, keep your oddments of wool, cut them into short lengths and leave around the garden. They're ideal for birds nest-building in your garden.

Superfood!

EAT MORE... AVOCADOS

Packed with...

Vitamins A, B, C and E, folic acid, fibre, potassium, iron, healthy monounsaturated oil, beta-sitosterol and lutein.

Good for...

Maintaining heart health, aiding digestion and boosting circulation. Can help prevent depression and fatigue too.

Get more by...

Making a delicious dip by mashing with olive oil, sliced black olives, lemon juice and finely chopped basil leaves. Serve with raw crudites or spread on to wholemeal bread. Chunks of avocado can also be added to cooked pizzas or soups.

In the kitchen

CARROT CAKE

Serves 12

- 250 ml (approx ½ pint) sunolive oil (a mixture of sunflower and olive oil)
- 225 g (8 oz) light muscovado sugar
- 3 large eggs
- 225 g (8 oz) self-raising flour
- 250 g (9 oz) carrots, coarsely grated
- Pecan halves

For the frosting
- 250 g (9 oz) mascarpone cheese
- 25 g (1 oz) unrefined golden icing cane sugar, sieve

1 Preheat the oven to 180°C, 350°F or Gas Mark 4. Grease and line a 20 cm (8 in) round tin with baking parchment.

2 Whisk the oil and sugar together, then whisk in the eggs one at a time.

3 Gently fold in the flour, followed by the carrots. Mix gently until combined, then turn into the prepared tin. Bake for 40 minutes until golden brown and a cocktail stick inserted into the centre comes out clean.

4 Cool in the tin for 10 minutes, then turn out and cool on a wire rack.

5 Mix together the mascarpone cheese and the golden icing sugar. Spread over the top and sides of the cake with a palette knife. Finish with pecan halves.

Recipe courtesy Billington's and Allinson

We remember when...

Concorde made its maiden flight on March 2, 1969, in France. It was hard to see just how huge the supersonic plane was from the newspaper and television reports, but for those of us who later saw the Concorde at an airport or flew in one, it was certainly a sight to behold. Concorde began commercial flights in 1976 and carried more than 2.5 million passengers by the time of its last flight in 2003.

A Grand Day Out

Doreen and her mother

When I was a child I lived in a small village with a Social Club and I was about six years old when one Saturday in the summer we went on a day trip to Southsea, on an old coach from White's Coaches.

We'd been travelling for a while when the coach pulled off the road, the boot was opened and all sorts of things appeared. My Dad's drum kit, two accordions, and my uncle pulled his mouth organ from his pocket.

So then the party started! People were singing, dancing and drinking bottles of pale ale, with port and lemonade for the ladies.

Everyone had brought a food package to share out. We had three Rhode Island Red chickens so we always made egg sandwiches.

After the picnic party, everything was packed back into the coach and off we went. Southsea was only about 60 miles away and we arrived about midday, to leave at 6.30pm – just enough time to have a paddle, a ride on the fair, fish and chips, and candy floss.

On the way home, we stopped at a pub and Mum put a dollop of ice-cream in my lemonade and told me it was an 'ice-cream soda' – very exciting! **Doreen Greener, Hull**

LEEDS ANCIENT AND MODERN

Grand civic heritage

Appropriately for the city that claims to be the Knightsbridge of the North, Leeds is where Michael Marks, the founder of Marks & Spencer, first set up his Penny Bazaar in 1884. Montague Burton, another famous high street name, opened the largest clothing factory in Europe in Leeds. Today, shoppers flock to the city's own branch of Harvey Nichols as well as the shops in its handsomely restored arcades. The Victorian era was Leeds' boom time so it is not surprising that it boasts some of the country's best architecture of that period. Designer Cuthbert Brodrick was responsible for two of the finest; the imposing Town Hall opened by Queen Victoria herself in 1858, and the Corn Exchange which now houses a variety of small shops and cafés.

Also housed in a distinguished Victorian building, once part of the city's famed St James' hospital (known affectionately as Jimmy's) is the Thackray Medical Museum.

For those who prefer a very different sort of

theatre, Leeds offers something for all tastes with its famous City Varieties Theatre, the Civic Theatre and the West Yorkshire Playhouse. The Grand Theatre is home to Opera North.

Although it celebrates its Victorian heritage, Leeds is very much a bustling modern city and one of its award-winning new buildings is the Henry Moore Institute which honours the memory of Yorkshire's best-known sculptor. History buffs won't want to miss the Leeds City Museum. Scheduled to open this year; it promises to show long-hidden collections that reveal the city's fascinating story.

Brass bands, by gum!
Mining was important in the village where Dilys Parry of Liverpool grew up

Our village

My village combined coal mining and farming. Mother was the district nurse and midwife and Father was a miner. Sometimes I used to go and watch my Father playing crown green bowls at the Miners' Institute. I would sit on a bench with a packet of crisps and a drink.

At other times I used to go with my mother to the baby clinic in the village and watch her weigh the babies. She was well loved by all. When she had to go out at night, she took her bag, torch and bike. Miners coming home would touch their caps and

say, 'Goodnight, Nurse'. Later, my mother had an A40 car with the registration NCA – known by all as Nurse Come Again.

Children in the village had a wonderful time. For six old pennies we went to the cinema

where each Saturday Mr and Mrs Davies showed Batman and Robin and cowboy films in their old wooden hut.

Sunday was kept as a special day for going to Sunday School.

Friday night was Brownie night and before that we changed our library books from the meagre supplies brought in boxes.

Once a year there was a village carnival. One old lady always collected the most money in her charity parade tin because everyone loved her. With her prize money of five shillings and her pension money she bought a small gift for every village child.

Next on the list...

Betty Kellar took a trip to see the River Severn's famed high tide – and found it anything but a 'bore'

My husband Alan and I, have a list of things we'd like to do, before we're too old. One of these was to see the Severn Bore, a tidal wave which races up the River Severn and is at its best when a high tide coincides with a full moon. So we hired a houseboat on the Severn and took my sister with us.

The houseboat had once been a Severn cargo ship, carrying goods from Avonmouth up to Gloucester. She's now moored on a purpose-built ledge in the river bank.

Mike, the boat owner, came to tell us that a good Bore was expected. Unfortunately, the first one was in the night, but the next was expected about midday the following day. "A lot of people come to see it," he told us. "You're welcome to invite a few on board if you like, but can you keep the number down? One family once let everyone come aboard and part of the deck fell in."

The Bore that came in the night was stupendous. We could see the water rushing by in the moonlight

and felt it lift the boat. We hadn't realised that the river rises for about an hour after the Bore has passed and we lay in our beds in the hull, listening to it rushing past the porthole and, thankfully, remembering the strong ropes that tied her to the mooring posts.

The water had also lifted the

We hadn't realised the river rises for about an hour

prow. So Alan's nocturnal visit to the loo, 75 feet along to the stern, was noticeably downhill there and uphill back.

We didn't see anyone come to watch the Bore in the dark, but the next day – a Sunday – we looked out of the porthole to see at least 100 people milling about on the Severn Way which ran past the boat.

The sight brought back an uneasy recollection. Mike had said we could invite a few on board – but what if they all wanted to come? How could we say: "You can come, but not you?" So we took the coward's way out – we skulked out of sight on the river side of the boat.

We saw the Bore coming around the bend of the river, just like a tidal wave. Little boats surfed it, together with water-skiers, all led by one intrepid boat which looked as though it would fall off the crest. But, of course, it didn't.

It was a wonderful holiday and another ambition achieved. The year before we'd had a Camping Coach on the North York Moors Railway – why had we never done that before?

This year, we've crossed another one off our list – halfway through our 70s and we'd never been to Stratford-upon-Avon to see a Shakespeare play. What next? A lighthouse. And we'd better do that while we can still get up and down the stairs!

Left: The crest of the Severn Bore
Right: After the Bore has passed
Above: Betty and Alan on board

Saturday

1
St. David's Day

Sunday

2
Mothering Sunday

Monday

3

Tuesday

4

Wednesday

5

Thursday

6
Crufts begins

Friday

7

Saturday

8

Sunday

9

Monday

10
Commonwealth Day

Tuesday

11
Yours magazine on sale
Yours Live Butlins, Skegness

Wednesday

12
National No Smoking Day
Yours Live Butlins, Skegness

Thursday

13
Yours Live Butlins, Skegness

Friday

14
Yours Live Butlins, Skegness

Saturday

15

Sunday

16
Palm Sunday

Monday

17
St. Patrick's Day (Bank Holiday, N Ireland)

Tuesday

18

Wednesday

19

Thursday

20
Maundy Thursday

Friday

21
Good Friday

Saturday

22

Sunday

23
Easter Sunday

Monday

24
Easter Monday (Bank Holiday, except Scotland)

Tuesday

25
Yours magazine on sale

Wednesday

26

Thursday

27

Friday

28

Saturday

29
Oxford/Cambridge Boat Race

Sunday

30
British Summer Time begins

Monday

31

PIC: REX FEATURES

Born this month

Daniel Craig, the sixth actor to play secret agent James Bond, was born on March 2, 1968, in Chester. His first Bond film was Casino Royale, released in 2006, and he received a BAFTA nomination for Best Actor for the role.

Married this month

Millions of teenage hearts were broken on March 12, 1969, as Beatle Paul McCartney married Linda Eastman at Marylebone Register Office, London. They were married for 29 years and became one of the most well-known couples in showbiz, until Linda's death from breast cancer in 1998.

Died this month

American film actor James 'Jimmy' Cagney (pictured), best known for playing gangster roles, died of a heart attack at the age of 86 on March 30, 1986.

A Grand Day Out

We were lucky enough to be one of the few families in our East London street to own a car in the 1940s, a second hand Morris Minor and - when petrol permitted - we'd usually take a trip to High Beech in Epping Forest.

Mum would pack a picnic and we'd trek through the woods until we came to a clearing which we called 'our glade' as we seldom saw anyone else picnic there.

Our favourite game involved Dad pulling us along on an old blanket over the grass, while we laughed and shouted for more. It's a wonder we weren't sick.

Sometimes Dad would stop at a pub on our way home and treat us each to lemonade and a packet of plain crisps, with that little blue packet of salt. Bliss!

Pat Rolfe, Hornchurch, Essex

Above: Pat, up to her ears in fern
Left: Pat still loves to walk in Epping Forest

Great gardening
Wallflower

If there's one spring-flowering plant that most gardeners recommend, it's the wallflower. Producing masses of colour early in the year, it's a real winner. Although you can buy plants at the garden centre, you can save yourself a few pounds by sowing them yourself. As they're biennial in habit, you need to sow seeds the previous summer for flowers in the spring. So, if you want to enjoy the lovely new variety 'Aurora' next March - its cheerful, sunrise-coloured flowers have a wonderful scent - then sow a few seeds between May and July this summer.

■ You can order it from Mr Fothergill's Seeds tel: 0845 1662511 or www.mr-fothergills.com

Superfood!

EAT MORE... PARSLEY

Packed with...

Calcium, iron and Vitamin C.

Good for...

Cleansing the blood, freshening breath and may help to clear kidney stones.

Get more by...

Adding to omelettes or mixing up your own parsley butter to serve with fish or meat - cream together 3 tbsp of butter with half a tbsp of lemon juice and 1 tbsp of finely chopped parsley.

In the kitchen

▓ BROCCOLI AND SMOKED SALMON TART ▓

Serves 4

- ■ 150 g (5 oz) tenderstem broccoli (8-9 spears)
- ■ 2 medium eggs
- ■ 2 medium egg yolks
- ■ 1 x 142 ml (approx 1/4 pint) carton single cream
- ■ 4 spring onions, finely sliced
- ■ Small handful of flat leaf parsley, chopped
- ■ Salt and pepper
- ■ 125 g (4 ½ oz) smoked salmon, chopped
- ■ 1 x 20 cm (8 in) baked shortcrust pastry case

1 Preheat the oven to 180°C, 350°F or Gas Mark 4. Cut the broccoli into pieces, so that each floret end is about 7-8 cm (3 in) in length. Roughly chop the stalk pieces. Cook the broccoli in boiling water for 4 minutes, rinse under cold water and set aside.

2 Mix together the eggs, egg yolks, cream, spring onions and parsley. Season with pepper and a little salt, if liked (the smoked salmon may add enough salt for you).

3 Arrange the smoked salmon and the chopped stalk pieces of broccoli in the baked pastry case. Pour the egg and cream mixture over. Arrange the floret end pieces of broccoli in the tart like the spokes of a wheel, with the florets around the edge of the tart.

4 Bake the tart in the preheated oven for about 25 minutes or until golden brown on top and just set.

5 Serve the tart with a green salad and a lemony dressing.   Recipe courtesy www.tenderstem.co.uk

▓ AROUND THE HOUSE ▓

If your old skirts and shirts aren't good enough to recycle, remember to cut out the zips and unpick the buttons to keep as spares in your sewing basket. And, depending on the material, you can recycle the clothes for rags or dusters.

My childhood home

A year ago I decided to find the house of my birth. Luckily, while gazing at the small terraced house in Warwick, a man asked if he could help me. I explained that I was on a nostalgic visit and that I was born in this house in 1938. He invited me in – how did we manage to have a piano and chairs in the small lounge? I remember we had Art Deco ceiling light bowls and ornaments.

The house cost £250 and was built on prison grounds.

Gooseberry bushes lined the tiny path and Mother made jam from these. There was a wooden garage at the back and Dad always had a car.

We lived near fields with watercress growing in the stream; barges sailed by on the nearby canal. We would go to the woods, full of primroses and bluebells, and have lovely picnics – these were happy, happy days.

Dad was called up and things in the house changed. From my tiny bedroom window, I saw the sky red with fire, as Coventry blazed.

I would walk from school some days alone, which was quite a walk. One day, when I was six, I couldn't open the back gate, and the wind caught in my throat as I cried. A kind neighbour took me in and I was never to go in the house again until last year. My mother had left.

Shirley Ann Randle, Beoworth, Warwks

We remember when...

The BBC announced this week in 1966 that it was beginning broadcasting in colour from the following summer. And right on schedule, the first colour pictures were broadcast from Wimbledon the following year. BBC1 and ITV followed suit in 1969, the highlight of that year watching the Apollo 11 spacecraft on its way to the moon, in colour.

In the kitchen

LAMB SHANKS WITH CIDER, APPLE, ROSEMARY AND BEANS

Serves 2
- 1 leek, cut into thick slices
- 2 sticks celery, cut into thick slices
- 2 cloves garlic, crushed
- 2 eating apples, peeled, cored and sliced
- 3 sprigs rosemary
- 2 lean lamb shanks
- 600 ml (approx 1 pint) cider
- Salt and pepper
- 400 g (14 oz) can cannellini beans, drained

1 In an ovenproof casserole dish place the leek, celery, garlic, apples and rosemary.

2 Place the lamb shanks on top and pour over the cider. Season with salt and pepper and cover with a lid.

3 Cook in preheated oven, 170°C, 325°F or Gas Mark 3 for 2 hours, or until meat is tender and falling from the bone.

4 30 minutes before the end of the cooking time remove the lid and add the cannellini beans. Mix well and return to the oven uncovered for the remaining cooking time.

Recipe courtesy English Beef & Lamb Executive

TOP TIP

A few grains of rice in your salt cellar will stop your salt from clogging up.

Melanie King, Sheffield

We remember when...

Film star Grace Kelly, who married Prince Rainier of Monaco in 1956, gave birth to her second child, a boy named Albert Alexandre Louis Pierre this week in 1958. She died in a car crash in Monaco in 1982, her husband in 2005. Monaco is now ruled by their son, Albert.

AROUND THE HOUSE

Use a really thick towel on your hair to remove as much water as you can before you dry it. Blow-drying time will be shorter and you'll save on energy and your electricity bill.

Superfood!

EAT MORE... BROCCOLI

Packed with...

Vitamin C, B3 and B5, iron, potassium, beta carotene, folate, fibre, calcium and iron.

Good for...

Boosting eye health and lowering the risk of heart disease. Also thought to help prevent stomach ulcers and gastric cancers. And may help protect against other common forms of cancer too, including cancers of the colon, breast, lungs, larynx and bladder.

Get more by...

Serving with carrot crudités and a hummus dip for a crunchy snack. Or making a tangy salad by mixing together chopped broccoli, grated carrot and orange segments – drizzle with salad dressing and a squeeze of orange juice.

My childhood home

I was born on my father's two-acre smallholding in Wallington, Surrey. My father had an orchard of apples, pears, plums and soft fruit.

I made mud pies and pushed my doll's pram around the earth paths. I tried to copy my older siblings by climbing trees and remember once falling from a branch. As I grew older I loved sitting in the apple tree and pretending I was a pirate in the crow's nest. On wet days in the house we'd slide down the stairs on trays, or dress up in clothes from the big trunk.

I slept in my parents' room for several years, then moved in with my sisters in the big double bed.

Left: Maisie and her mum in 1937
Above: Maisie's house, destroyed by a doodlebug

When I was nine, in 1944, our house was destroyed by a doodlebug and for four years we lived in a cottage near Boxhill, then moving back to those same two acres – not the same house, of course. There I lived until I married in 1958.

Maisie Dance, Purley, Surrey

A Grand Day Out

"Wakey, wakey! Time to get up." The clock said only 5am but then realisation dawned – today was Ideal Homes Exhibition day. Each year on a Saturday in March, my mother and I travelled the 30-odd miles to London to enjoy the delights of the huge exhibition.

I washed and dressed in the kitchen (it was the 1950s) before setting off on the mile-and-a-half walk to catch the 6.15am train.

The early start meant we could look forward to our annual treat of a cooked breakfast in a little café in London before catching the Underground to arrive at Olympia just as the doors opened.

We invariably made our way to the garden section first to study the beautifully designed gardens, soaking up the colours and scents of roses, violets, snowdrops and lilies – all growing alongside each other. Nothing could compare with the highlight of that early walk into the gardens.

The rest of the time was spent wandering around the stands, watching gadgets being put through their paces and sampling the titbits on offer, finally queuing to see the interiors of the specially built houses.

I imagined living in such luxury; at home we had no bathroom and an outside toilet. Here we saw colourful kitchens and shiny bathrooms.

By mid-afternoon the crowds made it difficult to see much, so Mum and I used to leave for home, tired but having thoroughly enjoyed our day out.

Pearl Walsh,
Barnstaple, Devon

Great gardening
Edwardiana

If you're a novice gardener, then the best place to start is with hardy annuals. These can be sown where you want them to grow and will tolerate frost, so there's no waiting until May to plant them outside. Pinks may sound a rather traditional choice, but they're great garden plants and the newest variety from Thompson and Morgan is no exception. Dianthus chinensis 'Edwardiana' produces well-branched, free-flowering plants, in sumptuous antique shades of red, rose and white. Sow a few in a shallow drill now and they'll create a lovely display that lasts all summer.

■ To order seeds, tel: 01473 688 821 or visit www.thompson-morgan.com

My childhood home

Five-year-old Moria in 1948

My parents, brother and I were made homeless in the war and we had to move into a prefab in Hillingdon, Middlesex. I was barely a toddler, and can remember going into it for the first time. It was new and empty, except for the kitchen, and my mother said: "Someone's left a scrubbing brush in the corner." She walked towards it and it moved – it was a hedgehog.

When I hear how cold the winter of 1947 was, I wonder how we coped in the prefab. There was a wood burning stove in the living room which heated the water and did its best to heat the room.

The photograph is of me in 1948. I'm in the front garden with my new bike, wearing my cowboy outfit – I was quite a tomboy.

The boy next door, who was a lot older than me, used to hang his air rifle target on the shed door (behind me in the photo). He was at the other end of a telling off (which he might still remember) when mum found me with the rifle, taking aim at the target.

Moria Sandcock, Sherbourne, Dorset

TOP TIP

Decant washing up liquid into an old hand wash dispenser bottle. You'll use less this way.

Mrs J Crawford, Oban, Argyll

In the kitchen

CHOCOLATE EASTER NESTS

Makes 8 - 12
- 80 g (approx 3 oz) butter
- 25 g (1 oz) Fruisana Fruit Sugar
- 25 g (1 oz) cocoa powder
- 110 g (4 oz) milk chocolate
- 2 tablespoons golden syrup
- 175 g (6 oz) cornflakes, crushed
- 110 g (4 oz) mini chocolate Easter eggs

1 Place the butter, Fruisana, cocoa powder, milk chocolate and golden syrup in a medium sized saucepan.

2 Place over a very gentle heat and melt together, stirring constantly to ensure the mixture doesn't burn.

3 Stir in the cornflakes and mix well.

4 Place large spoonfuls of the mixture onto greaseproof paper and shape into nests.

5 Allow to set for at least 2 hours.

6 Place mini Easter eggs in the nests and serve.

Recipe courtesy Fruisana

We remember when...

An announcement was made this week in 1964 to build three new cities in south-east England. Building work started in the 1970s and the new cities created were Milton Keynes, Basingstoke and Havant. There was a fear that if new houses and facilities weren't built, the rising population would lead to pressure on services and employment in and around London. Big expansions were also carried out in Ashford, Ipswich, Northampton, Peterborough, Swindon and Stansted.

Great gardening

Cranberry Burst

When children draw their first flower, it's typically a daisy. Small wonder then that daisy-like flowers remain popular throughout our lives. Although they span several families of plants, many of those grown in our gardens are part of the argyranthemum group, which hails mainly from the Canaries. The majority make great container plants during the summer and new varieties are always gratefully received. One of the newest on the market is 'Cranberry Burst' which produces strange spiky blooms above domes of finely cut silver-green leaves. Similar to a chrysanthemum in appearance, it reaches around 60cm in height and can be ordered from Suttons Seeds – delivery during April.

AROUND THE HOUSE

Save old toothbrushes to clean around the back of taps, on tile grouting and sink overflows. An old pastry brush is wizard for cleaning nooks and crannies which attract dust, such as DVD systems, the corners of television screens, computer keyboards and phones.

Superfood!

EAT MORE... EGGS

Packed with...

Protein, calcium, vitamins A, B2, B12, D and E, phosphorus and iron, plus cartenoids lutein and zeaxanthin.

Good for...

Improving concentration, memory and emotional balance and preventing blood clots. Also thought to protect eyes against degeneration and cataracts. The yolks are rich in Vitamin D, which helps to protect bones.

Get more by...

Folding into an omelette or whipping into a soufflé. Simply boiling and serving with soldiers is still a favourite.

A Grand Day Out

My father was born in Ulverston and when I was a small child we used to visit aunties there on Easter Sunday, which was always exciting.

When we were approaching the station, over the viaduct from Grange Over Sands, father would hand me his white handkerchief and I would wave through the window to let Aunt Hettie (who lived in a cottage at the side of the canal) know we would shortly be arriving – and, as father would say – 'to get cracking with the dinner'.

After dinner we would go to collect primroses in the woods nearby and also walk up Hoad Hill to roll hardboiled eggs, decorated by auntie, down the hill. Father would be waiting at the bottom and whoever won, would be presented with a new sixpence.

Going home, we felt so happy with our tiny bunches of primroses and decorated eggs, and already looking forward to our next visit in the summer.

Dinah Boston, Crewe, Cheshire

Dinah in 1930, with her new parasol

My childhood home

Christine's childhood home

I spent my early years in a quiet close near to the sea, not far from Bournemouth. Ours was a solidly built, early twentieth century three-bedroomed house.

We didn't have central heating, and I remember the coalman struggling up the drive, bent and black under his heavy sacks.

My brother and I played our games in the back garden – the house wall was great for bouncing balls against, but if we became too enthusiastic and balls went over the fence we had to go, in fear and trembling, and knock on Mrs Wright's door. 'Please can we have our ball back?' Mrs Wright was an old lady of uncertain temper…

Beyond the garden was a caravan site. Alberto Semprini owned a caravan there and we would watch him through the fence, sitting outside the caravan playing his piano.

Occasionally, I return to the close but it seems much smaller now, as does the house. I don't see any children playing on the green and there is no hopscotch chalked on the pavement.

**Christine Barrett,
Bournemouth**

Great gardening
Petunias

A staple of many hanging baskets, trailing petunias have come on in leaps and bounds recently. New varieties appear in garden centres almost yearly and, after the amazing success of the Surfinia and Million Bell types, a new variety is set to become just as popular. Combining the flower power of the Million Bells type with the performance of the Surfinias, Pinola petunias will providing an eye-catching display all summer long. This is one new plant that should not be missed.

■ Order online from Suttons Seeds at www.suttons-seeds.com

Superfood!

EAT MORE... BEETROOT

Packed with...

Vitamin C, folic acid, iron, magnesium, calcium, phosphorus and potassium.

Good for...

Detoxifying the gall bladder and liver and cleansing the intestines.

Get more by...

Grating into sandwiches and on to salads or blending up a smoothie with chunks of fresh pineapple – a great energy booster!

In the kitchen

SAUSAGE BIRYANI

Serves 2

- 225 g (8 oz) chipolata sausages
- 30 ml (2 tablespoons) curry paste
- 1 onion, thinly sliced
- 100 g (approx 4 oz) mushrooms, chopped
- 450 g (1 lb) pre-cooked packet rice or 150 g (5 oz) dried rice, cooked
- 60 ml (4 tablespoons) water
- 5 cm (2 in) cucumber
- 1 tomato, finely chopped
- 15 ml (1 tablespoon) fresh coriander, finely chopped

1 In a large non-stick wok or saucepan, fry the sausages with curry paste for 3-4 minutes.
2 Add the onion and mushrooms and cook gently for a further 4-6 minutes. Add rice and water and cook for 3 minutes. Stir in the cucumber, tomato and coriander.
4 Serve with poppadums or toasted naan breads and relish.

Recipe courtesy Sausage Week

AROUND THE HOUSE

If you have a computer, don't spend any more than four hours a day looking at the screen, and take a break to have a stretch at least every 30 minutes, however urgent the need to get down your life story!

We remember when...

A full-size ski jump – made from real snow – was built on Hampstead Heath, London, this week in 1950. The snow had been specially imported from Norway for a ski competition between Norway and Britain. Skiers could jump up to 90 feet (27 metres) and the landing at the end was made of soft straw. But the highlight of the day was the competition between Cambridge and Oxford universities. Some things never change…

Two-year-old Estella, feeding a piglet

I was brought up in London, with four brothers and two sisters. We didn't go on holiday but my school ran country holiday funds, paying weekly. When I was 10 years old I had the chance to go to Devon and I thought it was wonderful to see the animals in the fields. I stayed with the Chamberlains who had Derrick, Dennis and Estella.

Mr Chamberlain did the farm work and milked the cows and he gave me warm milk straight from the cows. I wasn't very keen but he told me it would do me good, as I was too thin.

The next year I went again but couldn't stay with the Chamberlains as the children had measles, so I stayed at their grandparents.

Mr and Mrs Harris took us to sell butter, cream and eggs at market.

I kept in touch with them over the years and in 1940, Mrs Chamberlain wrote to ask if I would like to stay. I stayed and worked in shops until I was called up at 19.

While staying at the farm near Tiverton, I met my future husband, Frank. He joined the RAF and we married in 1946 and had six children. We had a lovely life, all thanks to Mrs Chamberlain offering me a rest in the country.

Elsie Manning, Cullompton, Devon

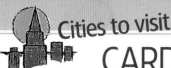
CARDIFF: ANCIENT AND MODERN

Tiger Bay transformed

One of the world's great seaports, Cardiff, is situated on the Bristol Channel. In 1955 it was proclaimed the capital city of Wales and on March 1st, 2006 the Queen opened the stunning modern building made of steel, slate and glass that is the seat of the Welsh Assembly. The building forms part of the city's massive regeneration programme for the twentyfirst century which has seen a transformation of the old dockside area known as Tiger Bay into Cardiff Bay.

Along Cardiff Bay's waterfront is Mermaid Quay, a complex of shops, restaurants and bars. Also in the Bay area is the Wales Millennium Centre which includes a 1,900 seat auditorium that is the home of the Welsh National Opera.

The Science Discovery Centre features 160 interactive exhibits as well as a Planetarium. While lovers of sport flock to the Millennium Stadium in the city centre, built on the site of Cardiff Arms Park where generations of rugby fans have sung, roared or groaned according to the fortunes of their teams.

This state-of-the-art construction has a retractable roof which makes it Europe's largest undercover venue for 72,000 spectators.

Ironically, the Welsh capital owed its development in the 19th century to a Scottish family, the Butes, who owned most of the valleys that were rich in coal. In 1839, the second Marquis of Bute began building the docks that made Cardiff one of the busiest ports in the world. The wealth created enabled the third Marquis to restore Cardiff Castle in an opulent Victorian neo-Gothic style that still draws gasps of wonder today.

Clip clopping along

Riding in a pony and trap was a treat for Letty Fitz of Bristol

Our village

I was so lucky to grow up in a Gloucestershire village where there was a village pond with dragonflies darting over the water. Goldfinches, yellow hammers and other small birds flew around.

Our house stood on an acre and a half of land which was a market garden. Every Thursday evening fresh produce was loaded on to a large wagon. I helped tie the rhubarb sticks and spring onions into bunches, wash new-laid eggs and clean fruit and vegetables ready for sale. Early Friday morning the wagon was pulled the seven miles to town by

Bonnie the shire horse.

My father kept pigs, goats, geese, chickens and pigeons. I helped my parents feed the livestock and loved collecting the eggs. There were two stables, cart sheds, pig styes and a chaff house. It was in the chaff house that corn and wheat was stored in large bins. One day I lifted the top of a bin and out jumped a fat mouse. My scream brought mother running and it was a long time before I went to the chaff house again.

We had a pony and trap for family use. One memorable ride was along the lanes lined with

wild flowers. I loved to see the primroses and cowslips and feel the fresh breeze on my face. The only sounds were the birds singing and the clip clop of the pony. We arrived at a farm where my father bought a cask of home-made cider that was always kept in the cupboard under the stairs.

On the village street I sometimes met a local 'celebrity', a vagabond who wheeled along a bicycle with a bunch of grasses stuck into the front lamp. Tom was a harmless, nature-loving man, who liked sleeping under the stars at the foot of haymows or in empty sheds.

The Rockin' Fifties

PIC: REX FEATURES

1 How many British families owned a car in 1950?
A 1 in 5
B 1 in 7
C 1 in 3
D 1 in 4

2 In which year did Roger Bannister become the first man to run a mile in less than four minutes?
A 1951
B 1955
C 1954
D 1958

3 Eddie Cochran (right) had his first British Top Ten hit in 1958. But which song was it?
A Three Steps To Heaven
B C'mon Everybody
C Twenty Flight Rock
D Summertime Blues

4 The Barbie doll was launched at The American International Toy Fair in?
A 1955
B 1957
C 1959
D 1951

5 The Royal Yacht Britannia was named and launched by the Queen in 1953. Where was the shipyard?
A Glasgow
B Belfast
C Liverpool
D London

6 American actor, Martin Landau's first major film role was in the Hitchcock classic?
A Vertigo
B North By Northwest
C The Wrong Man
D The Man Who Knew Too Much

7 In 1958 Britain's first parking meters were installed in which area of London?
A Mayfair
B Brixton
C Clapham
D Soho

8 Which famous fast food chain opened its first restaurant in 1955?
A Wimpy
B McDonalds
C Burger King
D Wendy's

9 The first episode of The Archers was transmitted in 1950. But which month?
A July
B April
C May
D June

10 The world's first nuclear submarine, Nautilus was launched in January…?
A 1950
B 1954
C 1955
D 1958

Answers: 1 B, 2 C, 3 D, 4 C, 5 A, 6 B, 7 A, 8 B, 9 D, 10 B

SEPARATE ROOMS

BY PENNY PECORELLI

Banished to the spare room for the night, Jane guiltily enjoys the luxury of solitude

It started with a nasty head cold. Jane snuffled and sneezed half the night. In the pitch dark of the early hours, she reached out for the glass of water at her bedside and knocked it over with a crash.

"Aargh," groaned Ken, switching on his bedside light. "I know you can't help having a cold, but I really need my sleep."

"Sorry, sorry!" muttered Jane, trying to mop up the water on the rug, "I'll go and sleep in the spare room."

Grabbing her book, her specs and her box of tissues, she pushed her feet into her soggy slippers, then crept out.

It was chilly in the spare room. By the time she'd adjusted the radiator, fetched a blanket from the airing cupboard and refilled her glass with water, she was wide awake. She read for a while, trying to blow her nose as quietly as possible. The pile of tissues grew higher and her nose much sorer before she eventually slept.

As they prepared for bed the following night, Jane told Ken: "I'll sleep in the spare room again," and noted the relieved look in his eyes. "Oh, well," he said, "If you must – just until you are feeling better."

Jane settled down into the warm bed. It really was quite a nice room this, she thought. With her box of tissues at hand, she opened her book, knowing she could read for as long as she wished without Ken pleading with her to turn off the light.

'I could get to like this', she thought, 'a room of my own – and no snoring from Ken. He complains about my snuffling but he makes more noise, especially when he's had a pint or two'.

She drifted off to sleep, snuggled cosily in the bed with nobody shifting restlessly beside her. She woke feeling refreshed:

'I could get to like this... a room of my own and no snoring

she hadn't slept so well in ages.

The next evening she announced: "I'm still a bit snuffly. I'll sleep in the spare room again, just in case."

Ken looked at her a bit oddly: "Okay, if you feel you need to."

This time she read until the small hours. It was a good book and it was a luxury to read for as long as she could keep her eyes open.

The next day her cold had gone so when Ken said at breakfast: "I've got a sore throat," she felt a twinge of guilt as her heart leapt at the prospect of sleeping in the spare room again. She was enjoying her self-imposed isolation.

By the end of the day, Ken had developed all the symptoms of a full-blown cold. Jane tucked him tenderly into bed with his supply of a hot toddy, tissues and ointment for his chest.

"You're not leaving me?" he asked pathetically. "What if I need anything during the night?"

"I'll only be in the spare room," she said, "I think it will be better if one of us gets a good night's sleep, don't you?"

Opening her book, she failed to feel the slightest bit guilty on hearing the honks and trumpeting from the other bedroom.

"How are you feeling, darling?" she asked solicitously the next morning, gently mopping his brow.

"Rotten," he replied, miserably.

"I'll bring you up some breakfast in bed," Jane said comfortingly.

So it was that they slept apart for two more nights. By then Ken's cold was better and she could no longer justify staying in the spare room.

Until the row.

It was really a very silly thing

'I suppose you're going off to the spare room again tonight?'

that started it.

Ken said, rather belligerently, "I suppose you're going off to the spare room again tonight?"

"Well, if you don't want me," she retorted – more sharply than she intended because she felt guilty at enjoying the peace and quiet. The tiff escalated, until Jane declared defiantly: "Well, I will then," and flounced off.

She started reading, but soon thoughts of Ken came into her mind. She suddenly missed curling up in his arms, feeling warm and secure.

She read on resolutely for half an hour, putting all thoughts of him out of her mind. He'd started the row; why should she give in?

Then in the distance she heard a rumble of thunder. It grew louder. She had hated thunderstorms since she was a child and used to hide under the bedcovers. She leaned over and opened the curtains a fraction just as a huge bolt of lightning flashed across the sky. Jane trembled.

Suddenly, there was a sound like the end of the world – a huge crack of thunder reverberated around the house.

Terrified, she leaped out of bed, knocking her book to the floor, and raced across the landing. She wriggled under the duvet and cuddled up to Ken.

"You're back," he said.

"Yes," she replied.

"I knew you would be when I heard the thunder," his voice held a smile.

She giggled: "Loud, wasn't it?"

"Nice to have you back," he said.

"Nice to be here," she replied, snuggling up against him, contentedly curling her body around his.

"Goodnight," Ken said.

"Goodnight," Jane replied and, as she drifted off to sleep, she thought that in a thunderstorm a good book was no substitute for a nice warm husband. She smiled to herself as she held him tightly.

TimSharville.com

April 2008

Tuesday

I
All Fools' Day

Wednesday

2

Thursday

3

Friday

4

Saturday

5

Sunday

6

Monday

7

Tuesday

8
Yours magazine on sale

Wednesday

9

Thursday

IO

Friday

II

Saturday

I2

Sunday

I3
Flora London Marathon

Monday

I4

Tuesday

I5

Wednesday

I6

Thursday

I7

Friday

I8

Saturday

I9

Sunday

20

Monday

2I
Queen Elizabeth's birthday (b. 1926)

Tuesday

22
Yours magazine on sale

Wednesday	Sunday
23 St. George's Day	27
Thursday	Monday
24	28
Friday	Tuesday
25	29
Saturday	Wednesday
26	30

PIC: REX FEATURES

Born this month

British actress Emma Thompson (pictured) was born on April 15, 1959, in Paddington, London. In 1996 she won her second Oscar, for her screenplay adaptation of Jane Austen's Sense and Sensibility. The first was for Best Actress, in Howard's End in 1992.

Married this month

Handsome American actor Burt Reynolds married actress Loni Anderson on April 29, 1988. It was Burt's second marriage and Loni's third, and they adopted a son, Quinton Reynolds, before a bitter divorce battle in 1995.

Died this month

Legendary Motown singer Marvin Gaye, who sung the 1969 chart-topping hit, I Heard It Through The Grapevine, died on April 1, 1984. He was shot dead by his father during a family argument.

My childhood home

I was born in an end terraced house in Featherstone, a small mining village in the West Riding of Yorkshire.

We had coal fire grates in the bedrooms and if the fire was lit, next door's bedroom fireplaces would smoke, so they knew someone was ill in bed and would come round to help.

We had gas lighting which had two chains either side, to light or to put out. When we went out on a dark night, we would pull one of them down to leave a low light on, so when we returned, the chain was pulled back to give us a bright light again.

**Mavis Hollis,
Pontefract, West Yorks**

We remember when...

A spaghetti bush became the most sought-after plant in Britain, on April 1, 1957, thanks to a joke by the BBC. A Swiss family were shown collecting their annual 'spaghetti harvest' from supposed spaghetti bushes on the programme Panorama, carefully placing the strands in the sun so they could dry…

Superfood!
EAT MORE... GARLIC
Packed with...

Manganese, Vitamins C, B6, B1, tryptophan, selenium, calcium, potassium, copper and phosphorus.

Good for...

Lowering blood pressure and helping prevent atherosclerosis and diabetic heart disease. Also thought to reduce the risk of stroke and give protection against some forms of cancer. Antifungal and antibacterial, good for relieving the symptoms of stomach bugs and chest infections.

Get more by...

Roast in olive oil, crush and add to mash potato, or mix into sauces, soups and salad dressings.

Great gardening
Begonias

When it comes to summer bedding, few plants beat the flower power of begonias – and there's a spectacular range called Tenellas. These produce an abundance of fringed double blooms, all of which hang elegantly from strong arching stems. Specially bred to have an upright habit early on, they compete better than other begonia varieties, so are never swamped by more vigorous plants. Once they've developed a strong framework they naturally start to trail, providing an abundance of colour throughout the summer.
■ Order from Suttons Seeds, or visit www.suttons-seeds.com

■ AROUND THE HOUSE

To clean a framed photograph, take it off the wall and lay it flat. Spray glass cleaner on a soft cloth and wipe the dust off. Don't spray the cleaner directly onto the glass, as it may leak through to the photograph.

In the kitchen

PASSION CAKE BARS
Makes 12 bars

- 2 large eggs
- 175 g (6 oz) light soft brown sugar
- 100 ml (3 $^1/_2$ fl oz) sunflower oil
- 225 g (8 oz) plain flour
- 2 teaspoons bicarbonate of soda
- 2 teaspoons ground mixed spice
- 1 teaspoon baking powder
- 225 g (8 oz) carrots, grated
- 100 g (3 $^1/_2$ oz) walnuts, chopped
- Zest and juice of 1 orange

To decorate
- 1 orange
- 25 g (1 oz) caster sugar
- 250 g (9 oz) tub quark or cream cheese
- 2 tablespoons icing sugar
- 1 tablespoon clear honey

1 Preheat the oven to 170°C, 324°F or Gas Mark 3. Oil a rectangular cake tin measuring 17 x 26 x 3 cm (6 $^1/_2$ x 10 x 1 $^1/_2$ inches). Line base with baking parchment.

2 In a large bowl whisk the eggs, sugar and oil together with an electric whisk until pale, thick and fluffy. Fold in the remaining ingredients and pour into the prepared tin. Bake for 35-40 minutes until risen and firm to the touch. Cool in the tin.

3 Meanwhile, use a potato peeler to thinly pare the zest from the orange and cut it into matchstick strips. Toss in caster sugar and leave to dry on greaseproof paper. To make the icing, beat the quark or cream cheese, icing sugar and honey together with 1 tablespoon of the orange juice and chill until required.

4 When the cake is cold, remove it from the tin and spread with the icing. Decorate with crystallised orange zest and cut into 12 bars. Chill until required.

Recipe courtesy Lion Quality Eggs

A Grand Day Out

A grand day out in 1937, aged nine, was with Uncle Ashley, Mother's older brother, a shy and eccentric bachelor.

My parents took over the family business, previously a tinsmith's shop run by Granddad and Uncle Ashley, but as an off-licence and general store.

We also had a number at Ringstead Co-operative store, so I was entitled to go on the annual children's trip to Wickstead Park, Kettering, 10 miles away.

After an exciting time on the swings and slides, and a lovely tea, my dear Uncle Ashley arrived on his bike and said: "I'm going to take you into town and buy you a bike." It cost £5, and they gave us discount for cash, and two new lamps.

If that wasn't enough excitement, we then went to Speights, the photographers. I'd not ridden a proper bike before and had to ride it the 10 miles back to Ringstead. It didn't bother me, as I was an adventurous child. However, the last few miles were ridden in the dark. When we eventually arrived home, Mother was very cross and Uncle Ashley left me at the door, as he was expecting a telling off, which I couldn't understand. But I can imagine her worry now. However, it had been a wonderful day.

Joyce Gunn, Whittlesey, Cambs

Joyce and Uncle Ashley – and the new bike!

In the kitchen

■ SALMON BITES ■

Makes 10

- ■ 110 g (4 oz) cream cheese
- ■ 40 g (1½ oz) walnuts, finely chopped
- ■ 1 tablespoon dill, chopped
- ■ ½ teaspoon Fruisana fruit sugar
- ■ Pinch cayenne pepper
- ■ 10 thin slices smoked salmon
- ■ Rocket leaves to serve

1 Stir the cream cheese to soften it, then stir in the walnuts, dill, Fruisana and cayenne pepper. Mix well.

2 Spread mixture onto salmon pieces and roll up. These should then be chilled until ready to use.

3 Serve on a bed of rocket leaves.

Recipe courtesy Fruisana

TOP TIP

A soft spectacle case is very useful in which to keep a mobile phone.

Vicki Thompson, Helston, Cornwall

A Grand Day Out

Although it was a dull morning as my husband and I boarded the coach for a trip to the Cotswolds, in 2002, our spirits were soon lifted by the driver's witty commentary!

There was an awful lot to see in a day, our first stop being to Burford, with its long wide street, full of antique shops, hotels and tea rooms.

Continuing on, we were driven down Kilkeny Hill, with its magnificent viewpoint of Cheltenham and Gloucester, admiring Gloucester Cathedral's beautiful stained-glass windows and ornate carvings. After a brief look around the city, it was time for a three-course lunch.

Back on our journey, we toured Cheltenham, home of horse racing and the Gold Cup, and on to the charming village of Winchcombe, snugly situated in a wooded valley, with its 8th century Abbey.

The Cotswolds are renowned for their pretty villages – the exquisite Broadway; Chipping Camden with its thatched cottages, tiny shops and an impressive wool church; pretty Lower Slaughter, with a tributary of the River Windrush winding through its ancient, two-arched bridge; and Upper and Lower Swell.

The sun finally appeared as we reached Bourton-on-the-Water. Here we looked around a perfume factory, a vintage car museum and – to my husband's delight – Birdworld with its collection of fine birds, including pink flamingoes.

We tucked into a cream tea and strolled by the river before boarding the coach for home, the driver taking us back through some lovely Oxfordshire villages.

I'd visited the Cotswolds before but never had I explored such interesting places.

Florence Scott, Hemel Hempstead, Herts

We remember when...

The Soviet Union won the first leg of the space race this week in 1961, as astronaut Major Yuri Alexeyevich Gagarin orbited the earth for nearly two hours. American president John F Kennedy congratulated the Soviet Union, but a month later declared that America would win the space race by landing a man on the moon and returning him safely back to Earth, by 1970.

Superfood!

Packed with...

Viatmins C, A and K, folic acid, potassium and beta-carotene.

Good for...

Fighting bad bacteria and thought to have
anti-cancer properties.

Get more by...

Scattering on to cereals or into natural yoghurt. Or liquidise
together 10 strawberries, a nectarine and two apples – a great
immunity-boosting thirst quencher.

AROUND THE HOUSE

To make your flowers last longer,
cut off any leaves below water
level, to prevent them rotting.
Change the water daily, keep them
out of direct sunlight and add an
aspirin to the water. Clean narrow-
necked vases with a scourer of
water and either crushed egg shells
or dry rice.

My childhood home

Ann's childhood home,
taken April 1964

I lived in a cottage in
Padetwood, North Wales,
from my birth in 1940 until
I married in 1959. Originally a
farm worker's cottage, it had
thick stone walls and a tin
sheeting roof. When it rained
heavily, the noise was deafening.
There were two rooms – a
kitchen cum living room and
bedroom with an attached
washhouse and outside toilet.

Inside it was very cold in
winter and in summer it was
always cool, even on the hottest
day. Until 1950 the water had to be
carried from a well, which
was situated at the bottom of a
steep hill.

At Christmas time, there
wasn't a lot of room, so we tied a
bunch of holly from a beam, and
we hung baubles from it.

Ann Edwards, Chester

Great gardening

Radish

Vegetable gardening has
become incredibly popular
in recent years, with sales of
vegetable seeds overtaking those
of flowers. One vegetable that's
really simple to grow is the radish.
An annual vegetable, in that its
lifecycle lasts just one year, it came
originally from China. Constant
selection procedures have led to
massive improvements in quality
and you can now enjoy radishes in
a range of colours.

■ Thompson & Morgan has hand-
selected a visually eye-catching
array of radishes, all with crisp,
white, delicious flesh. Seeds of
'Rainbow Mixed' can be ordered
by calling 01473 688 821 or
www.thompson-morgan.com

My childhood home

The Catherine Wheel pub

My home was a pub called The Catherine Wheel, in Drayton Street, St Leonard, which is near Dorchester, Oxfordshire. I was born in 1938 and lived there with my parents, Bessie and Jim 'Jock' Cuthbertson and my brothers Philip and Douglas.

The pub was always full to overflowing and every night our lullabies were Roll Me Over in the Clover, or She'll Be Coming Round the Mountain.

The air force were stationed at nearby Mount Farm. The Americans, too, were a big part of our lives. We quickly learned 'Got any gum, chum?'

The army had huge searchlights in the field opposite, and I vividly remember army tanks in our back garden. The soldiers used to wake us early in the morning with huge tin plates of porridge and condensed milk.

I remember the winter of 1947 – we had an outhouse where the stock was kept. One night there was a loud bang, followed by more strange sounds. My father discovered that all the lemonade bottles had exploded with the severe frost.

I will never forget my charmed childhood and have such happy memories – I wonder if anyone remembers The Catherine Wheel as it was all those years ago?

**Daphne Prentice,
Abingdon, Oxon**

We remember when...

The world's most famous ship, the Royal Yacht Britannia was launched from Clydesdale on April 16, 1953, in pouring rain, by Queen Elizabeth II and the Duke of Edinburgh. It was one of the Queen's first engagements as Monarch; she'd officially become Queen in February. Britannia sailed for 44 years, but made her last voyage in January 1997. She's now permanently moored in the port of Leith, in Edinburgh.

In the kitchen

■ BERRIES AND CREAM PAVLOVA ■

Serves 8
- 3 large egg whites
- 175g (6oz) caster sugar
- 1 teaspoon cornflour
- 1 teaspoon vanilla essence
- 1 teaspoon white or red wine vinegar

Filling
- 300ml (approx ½ pint) double cream
- 110g (4oz) blueberries
- 150g (5oz) strawberries, hulled and halved

1 Preheat the oven to 130°C, 250°F or Gas Mark 1/2. Line a baking sheet with baking parchment and draw a 23 cm (9 in) circle in the centre.
2 Whisk the egg whites in a grease-free bowl until they form stiff peaks. Add half the caster sugar and whisk again until the mixture is thick and shiny. Mix the cornflour, vanilla essence and vinegar to a paste and fold in the eggs with the remaining sugar.
3 Pile the meringue into the circle on the baking sheet, making a hollow in the centre. Bake for about 1½ hours or until pale brown but a little soft in the centre. Leave to cool.
4 Whip the cream until it forms soft peaks, heap in the centre of the meringue and top with the fruit. Serve within 1 hour of filling.

Recipe courtesy Lion Quality Eggs

▌ TOP TIP ▐

Tape flat car air-fresheners onto the inside of your wheelie bin, which will keep it smelling fresh for weeks.

Brenda Dobson, Whitby, N Yorks

Great gardening

Pacific Night

One of the newest shrubs available to gardeners is Coprosma 'Pacific Night' which has glossy, maroon, evergreen leaves. Really intense in colour, these provide a remarkably striking contrast when grown alongside other plants, especially those with gold, silver or green leaves. Recently introduced by Notcutts, this pretty shrub, whose relatives are natives of Australasia, has a dense upright habit, making it ideal in containers. Reaching 1m in height, it's available from Notcutts Garden Centres. Visit www.notcutts.co.uk

AROUND THE HOUSE

If you're decorating and kicking up dust (sanding paintwork, for instance) spray a mist of water into the air with your plant sprayer to settle the dust.

Superfood!

EAT MORE... WATERCRESS

Packed with...

Vitamin C, calcium, phosphorus, beta-carotene, potassium, iodine and magnesium.

Good for...

Stimulating the thyroid, purifying the blood and breaking up kidney or bladder stones.

Get more by...

Mixing with chopped nuts, balsamic vinegar and olive oil for a tasty healthy salad. A perfect addition to egg sandwiches.

A Grand Day Out

Pauline, wellies on, with Sooty

I travelled to Canvey Island, my grandparents' home, with Mum and Dad, on their motorbike and sidecar in the 1950s. Then I borrowed Nan's bike and cycled around the island, usually ending up at the amusement arcade and indulging in putting in a few pennies at my favourite fruit machine.

I had an uncle only three years older than me and would hang around him, longing for him to take me out in his rowing boat to fish in the estuary together.

During the winter months I would pester Nan to unlock the piano in the front room so I could pretend to be a famous concert pianist. They were none too pleased to do so, as that was where they kept their rent money and pension books.

The best day out was when Nan and I would put on our Wellingtons and (along with Sooty, Nan's black and white spaniel) we'd climb over the old Dutch wall between the coastal lane and the beach, then splodge in the mud turning over rocks in search of winkles and cockles.

When we'd filled the buckets, we'd walk the mile home, our boots and legs covered with mud, which was part of the fun.

The winkles were a wonderful treat for Granddad, and I would watch fascinated as the older two prised out the insides with a needle and swallowed them, one by one. I could never understand the attraction and stuck to my bread and jam.

Linda Hurdwell, Ascot, Berks

A Grand Day Out

Great gardening

Astrantia

Although natives of the European Alps, astrantias have always been popular in the UK because they make great cottage garden plants, coping in sun or partial shade, and thriving in a variety of soils. Now Hayloft Plants has added a new variety, 'Venice', to its catalogue alongside 'Snowstar' and 'Roma'. Producing masses of claret-coloured, papery blooms, on plants around 90cm in height, it will create plenty of impact in your borders.

■ To order plants, tel: 01386 554 440 or www.hayloftplants.co.uk

AROUND THE HOUSE

Don't forget to save your plastic water bottles to use as mini cloches to protect your tender seedlings and plants from potential April frosts. Bubble wrap is a good protector, too.

Joan (left) and Joyce at Rhyl in the 1930s

My first memory of a holiday was from our home in Wolverhampton, to Rhyl in North Wales, for a day trip with our mothers.

Joan and I met as small children. I was one of six and she was an only child, so she spent a lot of time at our house. How exciting it all was to visit the seaside, and you must agree our costumes are very becoming!

We are now in our mid eighties and both widowed, and are still friends. Joan lives in Devon and I live in Wallasey and over the years we have visited each other with our families.

I have visited many places in the world but as I sit here in my lovely little flat overlooking the mighty Mersey, I often think of our first day trip to sunny Rhyl.

Joyce Birch, Wallasey, Merseyside

Superfood!

EAT MORE... MUSHROOMS

Packed with...

Vitamins B3 and B5, folic acid, zinc, magnesium, calcium and iron.

Good for...

Boosting the immune system, lowering cholesterol and thinning the blood.

Get more by...

Threading on to skewers with chunks of red pepper, red onion and cherry tomatoes. Brush with olive oil and grill before serving with your favourite fish or meat.

In the kitchen

■ ST GEORGE'S STILTON-TOPPED BEEF STEAK ■

Serves 2
- ■ 12.5 g (½ oz) butter
- ■ 15 ml (1 tablespoon) olive oil
- ■ 3 cloves garlic
- ■ 1 slice bread, crust removed and cut into quarters
- ■ 2 flat mushrooms or 4 standard mushrooms, cut into thick slices
- ■ 2 lean beef sirloin, fillet or rump steaks
- ■ 45 ml (3 tablespoons) fresh flat leaf parsley, chopped
- ■ 45 ml (3 tablespoons) crème fraîche
- ■ Salt and black pepper
- ■ 50 g (2 oz) Stilton cheese

1 Heat the butter, 10 ml olive oil and 1 clove crushed garlic in a frying pan. Add the bread and cook for 1-2 minutes each side until it resembles croutons. Remove from pan with any cooked garlic pieces.

2 Spoon the remaining 5 ml (1 teaspoon) olive oil into the pan and heat. Add the remaining 2 cloves of crushed garlic, the mushrooms and the beef steaks. Cook for 3-4 minutes (rare), 4-5 minutes (medium) and 5-6 minutes (well done).

3 Meanwhile, in a small bowl mix together the parsley and crème fraîche. Season with salt and pepper. Top the cooked beef steaks with garlic mushrooms, Stilton cheese and garlic croutons. Drizzle with the crème fraîche and parsley.

Recipe courtesy English Beef & Lamb Executive

We remember when...

The shilling and florin were replaced by the new five and ten pence coins this week in 1968. Many people were confused by the first step towards decimalisation and refused to take the coins. The change to the new system happened gradually over three years, until Decimal Day, on February 15 1971, when shillings ceased to exist altogether.

My childhood home

Pat's brother outside their house

I grew up in the late 1940s, early 1950s, in a tenement house in North London. My parents, sister, brother and me lived in two living rooms and scullery in the basement and two bedrooms on the first floor. Two other families lived on the two stories above us. We all shared a small backyard where each family had their day for hanging out the washing.

Our toilet was just outside the back door, next to the coal cellar. One day the coalman opened the basement door and shouted: "Coal!" "Come in," Mother replied, and he opened the toilet door. I don't know who was more shocked, Mum or the coalman!

From our front window we had a clear view of anyone coming to the front door – particularly useful when Mum didn't have the rent money and it gave us time to hide behind the settee until he'd gone.

The house always seemed very dark, so every night in winter I'd run upstairs, swinging my hot water bottle into the dark recesses, so as to stun any bogeymen.

The fuse boxes for the street were in the first floor hall. It was common for the lights to fail and, rather than calling anyone out, Dad would repair it himself. On one occasion, he couldn't fix it so the repairman came. As he poked in the fuse box, there was a sharp intake of breath, 'I don't know who's done this, but they should be arrested for it'. No one said a word but Mum took us to one side and whispered: "Don't say anything." It didn't stop Dad from doing his own repairs in the future.

Pat Gregory, Bricket Wood, Herts

NORWICH: ANCIENT AND MODERN

Here be dragons

Norwich claims to be the most complete medieval city in Britain and cobbled Elm Street, with its beautifully preserved timber-framed houses, has changed little in the past 500 years. One of the city's many small museums is Dragon Hall, a fifteenth century merchant's house featuring an intricately carved dragon recently restored to its former glory.

A maze of ancient streets and alleyways – Lower Goat Lane, Pottergate and St Benedict's Street – attract shoppers in search of everything from fashion to books and antiques. The Royal Arcade is a covered shopping area in the art nouveau style that was popular in the 1890s when it was built. Here visitors can buy one of the city's most famous products in Colman's Mustard Shop. Close to the Arcade is a huge open-air market that is open six days a week.

Overlooking the recently revamped market is the Norman Castle which houses the works of the Norfolk school of watercolour painters including

John Sell Cotman, a native of the city.

Dominating the city is its magnificent cathedral and Close which can be admired over a cup of tea and cake in the Refectory Restaurant. A short stroll takes you down the River Wensum and the picturesque old watergate known as Pull's Ferry which was no doubt a familiar sight to Norfolk's most famous son, Admiral Nelson, who attended a school in the grounds of the Close.

The largest of Norwich's medieval churches, St Peter Mancroft, can be admired from the city's most modern and architecturally stunning Forum.

Steamed pud and golden syrup

School dinners weren't so bad says June Gale of Farnborough, Hampshire

Our village

Until the age of 23, I lived in a bungalow halfway between the two villages of Frimley and Frimley Green. Opposite my home were the village schools. Aged five, I started at the infants. When we were seven, we were moved to the senior school next door.

The canteen was in the village hall next to the school. During the Second World War, our meals were made more interesting by gifts from Canada of large rolls of steamed pudding to which was added golden syrup and rather watery custard. This was much appreciated by the ever-

hungry boys, always eager for second helpings.

School days were interrupted by air raid sirens when we had to troop down into the concrete shelters built on the playground. They were cold, damp and dingy places but we had to try and continue our lessons.

Cars were few and far between. I only knew of two; one owned by the vicar and one by the doctor. The boys would play football on the road, just stepping aside if a car came along.

Local characters included a little old lady who dressed entirely in black. She wore a hat

and had swarthy skin and black hair. We children would cross the road when we saw her coming as she would stare and mutter at us.

The local garage owner was a grumpy man who used to hiss when we turned up with accumulators to be charged. These were batteries for our radios; sealed glass boxes filled with acid. They had to be handled with care but I was allowed to hang two of them on the handlebars of my bike, carefully riding the half-mile to the garage.

PIC: REX FEATURES

Swingin' Sixties

1 What does the 'T' in Captain James T Kirk stand for?
A Travis
B Tiberius
C Thomas
D Terence

2 What was Paul McCartney's first car?
A Ford Anglia
B Ford Consul Classic
C Ford Corsair
D Ford Cortina

3 How many times did Henry Cooper and Muhammad Ali meet in the boxing ring?
A Once
B Three times
C Twice
D Never

4 In 1963, John Profumo resigned, due to the scandal surrounding his involvement with a prostitute. What was his government post?
A Home Secretary
B Education Secretary
C Health Secretary
D Secretary of State for War

5 In the film 'Alfie' what was the name of Jane Asher's character?
A Annie
B Ruby
C Lily
D Gilda

6 In which year were betting shops made legal in Britain?
A 1960
B 1963
C 1961
D 1965

7 Which newspaper launched Britain's first colour supplement magazine?
A The Sunday Times
B The Daily Mail
C The Sun
D The Sunday Express

8 What is Twiggy's (pictured) real name?
A Lesley Lawson
B Lesley Hornby
C Elizabeth Norman
D Helen Hornby

9 In which year did American scientist, Theodore Maiman, invent the Laser?
A 1960
B 1965
C 1961
D 1968

10 In Disney's 'The Jungle Book', who voiced King Louis?
A Louis Armstrong
B Sammy Davis Jr
C Phil Harris
D Louis Prima

Answers: 1 B, 2 B, 3 C, 4 D, 5 A, 6 C, 7 A, 8 B, 9 A, 10 D

KNOWING MR RIGHT

BY BARBARA O SMITH

Is Chris really ready to change her life for ever?

"It will all work out right in the end," Chris told herself, although she wasn't quite sure whether she believed it. The mobile phone in the pocket of her 'seen better days' gardening jacket rang, distracting her from pruning the forsythia. Throwing down the secateurs, she tugged her gardening gloves off with her teeth and pressed the button.

"Hello, Nicholas," she said and then, after listening intently, exploded, "I don't believe a word of it, you're making it up!" Cursing her old friend for putting such awful doubts into her head, she stabbed the 'off' button angrily.

Chris examined the dark crescents of compost beneath her fingernails and sighed. How did soil manage to get through gardening gloves? There had been a time when her hands were soft and her nails manicured. The passage of time, housework, children and gardening had changed that. Now they were brown and rough, nobbly with the onset of arthritis.

Her tights were laddered by brambles and her hair was speckled with leaves. But her sorry appearance didn't bother her, life was too short to fret over her looks, and anyway, Gordon said he liked her the way she was. She walked slowly up the garden, head bent in thought, hoping that everything would work out well in the end.

Chris showered, towelled her hair dry and brushed it into soft pearly grey waves. Rubbing cream

Life was too short to fret over her looks...

into her hands, she glanced at the smart powder blue suit hanging on the wardrobe door. It was the most expensive outfit she had bought in years. She knew it was impractical for her lifestyle, but every time she looked at it, she felt a delicious thrill at its sheer extravagance.

She picked up the bottle of nail varnish from her dressing table. She hadn't painted her nails for ages. Varnish couldn't hide the wear and tear of her workworn hands, but it did disguise the rough nails, and it looked pretty. She should do it more often, she decided.

When she was dressed, she stood in front of the mirror. "That's not the real me," she said to her reflection. The gracious lady looking back at her was far removed from the Chris of an hour ago. The image didn't feel right.

Would she have to change herself to fit in with Gordon's idea of what she should be like? He'd told her he loved her just as she was, but she couldn't forget his slight frown when he looked around her comfortably cluttered kitchen, with its stack of newspapers and letters on the table, the cup with the broken handle full of wild violets, her muddy wellies by the door.

The sound of laughter in the hall told her the children had arrived, reminding her that today she would cease to be their father's widow and become Gordon's wife. She took a last

look at the stranger in the mirror, picked up her gloves and went downstairs.

Jamie gave a wolf whistle. "What have you done to yourself. Mum? You look ..." he searched for the word, "glamorous."

"Don't be so old-fashioned, Jamie," his sister Naomi chided, "Mum, you look great, you really do."

Chris blushed. Her knees felt shaky; she needed to sit down, but the thought of creasing her skirt made her stand to attention. Chris had hoped a spot of gardening would have calmed her nerves, but now panic took hold. Surely there could be no truth in what Nicholas had said on the phone?

The church was beautifully decorated and Gordon looked very distinguished in his morning suit. Yes, of course everything would work out. She took her place by his side.

The vicar droned routinely: "If any of you know cause or just impediment why these persons should not be joined together…"

A female voice shouted from the back of the church.

"I do! He's married to me."

Afterwards, Chris was not sure whether her tears were of humiliation or relief. Nicholas had looked desperately sad for her, and she felt guilty that she hadn't believed him.

"I would have told you in a kinder way than blurting it out on the phone, but I'd only just found out and wanted to warn you before it was too late."

"He wasn't right for me, anyway," Chris assured him.

The blue outfit was wrapped in tissue paper and put away. Chris slipped comfortably back into her old routine.

One day Nicholas arrived as she was watering the tomatoes in the greenhouse. He stood watching her for a few moments before tapping on the glass. She looked up and smiled; Nicholas always brightened her day. She had known him for years; they were on the same wavelength, they laughed at the same things, shared the same taste in music.

Without preamble, he said: "I've been thinking about what you said, and I was wondering if I might be the one who is right for you."

Chris put down the watering can and stared at him. He had never told her he loved her, so she had never thought of him in a romantic light, which was a pity, because suddenly she knew he would be just right for her – and she for him. In reply, she wordlessly held wide her arms.

Thursday

1
Ascension Day

Friday

2

Saturday

3

Sunday

4

Monday

5
Early May Bank Holiday

Tuesday

6
Yours magazine on sale

Wednesday

7

Thursday

8

Friday

9

Saturday

10

Sunday

11
Pentecost (Whitsun)

Monday

12

Tuesday

13

Wednesday

14

Thursday

15

Friday

16

Saturday

17

Sunday

18
Trinity Sunday

Monday

19

Tuesday

20
Yours magazine on sale

Wednesday

21

Thursday

22

Friday

23
St. George's Day

Saturday

24

Sunday

25

Monday

26
Spring Bank Holiday

Tuesday

27

Wednesday

28

Thursday

29

Friday

30

Saturday

31

PIC: REX FEATURES

Born this month

George Lucas, famous for the epic Star Wars and action-packed Indiana Jones films, was born on May 19, 1944, in Modesto, California.

Married this month

American actor Humphrey Bogart married beautiful film and stage actress Lauren Bacall on May 21, 1945. She was 20 years old while Humphrey was 45. They stayed together until his death in 1957.

Died this month

American actress Rita Hayworth (pictured) died on May 14, 1987. She had been suffering from early-onset Alzheimer's disease since the age of 42, and was cared for by her daughter until she died.

My childhood home

Pamela's childhood home

The photograph shows the cottage in which I was born, although, at that time, it was only the area to the left of the door and was a one-up, one-down. There was a small scullery in which my mother cooked on an oil-stove and/or primus stove. Water for baths was heated in a galvanized tub on the primus stove.

There were six cottages, the toilets for which were 25 to 50 yards away (depending on which cottage you lived in).

I loved helping my father draw water from the nearby well before outside taps were installed in the 1950s. Electricity was also laid on about then and my grandmother, who was in her 80s, would light her oil lamp to see to switch on the electric light.

Pamela Hosey, Almayate, Malaga, Spain

Great gardening

Dierama

One catalogue that's always full of unusual plants is Ray Brown of Plant World Seeds, and he's introduced a showy plant called Dierama erectum, which hails from South Africa. Better known as Angel's fishing rods, dieramas are a wonderful choice and this species especially so, producing crowded stems of sherbert pink flowers during the summer. It reaches around 1.5m in height, but is only borderline hardy so make sure you cover it with a thick mulch during the winter.

■ To order seeds, tel: 01803 872 939 or visit www.plant-world-seeds.com

Superfood!

EAT MORE... OILY FISH

(herrings, tuna, salmon and mackerel)

Packed with...

Omega-3 essential fatty acid, Vitamin D and niacin.

Good for...

Enhancing brain function and lifting depression. Can also reduce cholesterol levels and help prevent heart disease and stroke. Also essential for strong bones and relieving the symptoms of arthritis.

Get more by...

Flaking into pasta dishes and salads or pan-frying with a squeeze of lemon and a sprig of dill.

AROUND THE HOUSE

To remove candle wax on clothes, put the item in the freezer for a while – you'll be able to crack the pieces off. If there's not too much to remove, lay a piece of brown paper and iron over it with a warm iron, which will melt and absorb the wax.

In the kitchen

▌ LIME AND COCONUT CRUNCHIES ▌

Makes 6
- 50 g (2 oz) butter, softened
- 75 g (3 oz) icing sugar
- Zest and juice of 2 limes
- 1 large egg
- 100g (3½ oz) plain flour
- ¼ teaspoon baking powder
- 50 g (2 oz) dessicated coconut

To decorate
- 25 g (1 oz) large coconut shreds
- 65 g (approx 2½ oz) icing sugar

1 Preheat the oven to 180°C, 350°F, or Gas Mark 4. Lightly oil two baking sheets.

2 Cream the butter and icing sugar together until fluffy. Reserve 1 tablespoon of the lime juice. Add the remaining lime juice, zest, egg, flour, baking powder and dessicated coconut and mix well to form a soft dough.

3 Place six spoonfuls of the mixture well apart on each of the baking sheets. Flatten with a fork and sprinkle over the coconut shreds. Bake for 10-12 minutes until golden. Cool on a wire rack.

To decorate

Mix the reserved lime juice with the icing sugar to make a thin icing. Drizzle the icing over the biscuits. Leave to set. These biscuits can be stored in an airtight container for up to 3 days.

Recipe courtesy Lion Quality Eggs

We remember when...

The musical My Fair Lady, starring Julie Andrews as Eliza Doolittle, opened in London on April 29, 1958 at the Drury Lane theatre. The first night was watched by stars such as Ingrid Bergman, Dirk Bogarde and playright Terence Rattigan. My Fair Lady broke all existing box office records.

A Grand Day Out

Mary on the right in those shoes

During a school year reunion in May 2004, I was presented with this photograph taken by a fellow pupil 50 years previously.

It showed a small group of windswept fifth form girls waiting at Swanage for a ferry to Bournemouth, during the annual school outing. For me it brought back both the pleasure and pain of that trip.

Always something of a rebel with regard to school uniform, I decided that, as I should be leaving school soon anyway, I would wear my new two-inch heel shoes. However, it was to prove 'pride before a fall'...

When I arrived at Bristol Temple Meads Station, the platform was heaving with 500 excited pupils ready for a trip to Dorset. The first stop was Bradbury Rings, then to Lulworth Cove for a picnic lunch.

I don't remember that bit of the trip, maybe because I was beginning to experience increasing discomfort from my footware.

The last hour spent exploring Bournemouth was absolute agony. I didn't take my shoes off on the return journey – what if I couldn't get them on again? What a relief when I finally reached my front door. It took my feet four or five days to recover.

I still, occasionally, indulge my love of smart high-heeled shoes at the expense of comfort!

Mary Kingdon, Bristol

In the kitchen

CHILLI NACHOS

Serves 4

- 450 g (1 lb) lean minced beef, minced lamb or pork
- 410 g (approx 14 ½ oz) can chick peas or red kidney beans, drained
- 500 g (1 lb 2 oz) jar chilli con carne sauce
- 150 g (5 oz) tortilla chips
- 30 ml (2 tablespoons) low-fat Cheddar cheese, grated

1 Place the mince in a large non-stick wok or saucepan and dry fry for 4-6 minutes, until browned.

2 Add the chick peas or red kidney beans, and the chilli con carne sauce and simmer for a further 6-8 minutes.

3 Place the tortilla chips in a bowl, pour the chilli mince over top and sprinkle with grated low-fat Cheddar cheese.

Recipe courtesy www.meatmatters.com

TOP TIP

Left-over tea is a really good tonic for roses and other plants.

Margaret Rowling,
Newton Aycliffe

A Grand Day Out

Below: Bridget and her sister Elizabeth (second and third left) and friends enjoying opening day at Desborough Park

In 1939, outings were severely restricted; London was out due to enemy bombardment, and petrol was rationed, so no trips to the seaside.

However, Lord Desborough, a general local benefactor, had given land for a new park to be created in Maidenhead, also for a scout hut nearby. We watched in awe as majestic structures were put up in the park – swings, a slide, a roundabout and a rocking horse – and we were impatient to try them.

In March 1939 the Mayor and Lord Desborough opened the 13th Maidenhead Troop scout, then returned in May to open Desborough Park. I was three, and had three older sisters of 11, 7 and 5, and a baby brother.

A daily outing to the park was a magical experience for us, a wonderland on our doorstep. We fell off the swings, banged our heads on the roundabout and grazed our knees when we fell down on the rough tarmac – a big sticking plaster was a badge of honour!

We took picnics – jam sandwiches and diluted welfare clinic orange juice – and had a box of dressing up clothes for rainy days, which we took to the park shelters where we staged plays.

We climbed trees, we collected conkers and the more studious children would sit by the railway track and collect GWR engine numbers and names. And the cost – precisely nothing.

Bridget Hole,
Maidenhead

We remember when...

The Second World War finally ended on May 7, 1945, as Germany signed an unconditional surrender after six long years of fighting. The Prime Minister, Winston Churchill broadcast a message to the British nation and cheering crowds dressed in red, white and blue gathered outside Buckingham Palace. The day was declared a national holiday, but the war in Japan continued for a further four months.

Superfood!

EAT MORE... CHERRIES

Packed with...

Vitamin C, calcium and phosphorus.

Good for...

Relieving headaches and fighting gout. This natural antiseptic also has antispasmodic qualities.

Get more by...

Blending up 4 handfuls of cherries with a pineapple – great for your skin and digestion. Cherries also make a delicious base for a crumble.

AROUND THE HOUSE

Hats attract dust, so keep them looking good by vacuuming them at the lowest suction setting now and again. Protect the trimmings by tucking a cloth round them.

Great gardening
Marshmallow

Few plants are more elegant than zantedeschias and the new variety 'Marshmallow' is delightful, producing beautiful pearl-white flowers with a delicious pink throat above lush, deep green leaves. Like all zantedeschias, it thrives in large containers or in a moist semi-shaded border, but looks best when grown at the edge of a pond. And, if you enjoy flower arranging then this really is a plant for you, because the flowers are excellent when cut. 'Marshmallow' produces an upright clump of leaves and will grow in sun or partial shade, as long as there's plenty of moisture.
■ It's available from Notcutts Garden Centres.
Visit www.notcutts.co.uk

My childhood home

Between 1940 and 1954 my sister Margaret and I lived happily with our parents at 71 Aviemore Way, Beckenham, Kent. Despite the war years, with memories of Mum running down the garden path to the shelter carrying food, and an incendiary bomb being found in our roof, we remember a great community spirit, with neighbours caring about one another – the VE Day party being one example of this.

In 2007 we were, unexpectedly, invited back by the present owners and spent a nostalgic morning remembering the large apple tree and shelter in the garden, now no more, standing in the bedroom we had shared during those years, and recalling the childhood fun we'd had. There is something very special about those early memories that never go away.

Janet Lambert, Longfield, Kent

Above: Janet outside her house in Beckenham
Top: Janet (right) and her sister Margaret in 2007

My childhood home

George and Jemima, around 1886

2 Great
Salterns
Cottages
today

In the kitchen

▓ ORANGE CHOCOLATE MOUSSE ▓

Serves 2
- ■ 50 g (2 oz) plain chocolate
- ■ 2 oranges
- ■ 150ml (¹/₄ pint) double cream
- ■ 2 tablespoons Grand Marnier liqueur
- ■ 2 teaspoons Fruisana fruit sugar

1 Break the chocolate into a bowl. Place over a pan of simmering water until melted, stirring occasionally. Allow to cool.

2 Grate the zest from one orange and stir into the cooled chocolate. Add 1 tablespoon each of Grand Marnier and Fruisana and mix together

3 Whip the cream until it is stiff and holds its shape. Gently stir into the chocolate mixture and mix well.

4 Divide into two glasses. Chill until required.

5 Peel and slice the oranges. Place in bowl and sprinkle with the remaining Fruisana and Grand Marnier. Leave to soak for 30 minutes before serving with the mousse.

Recipe courtesy Fruisana

Number 2, Great Salterns Cottages, Portsmouth is where I spent the first few years of my life. The cottages were built in 1882 and my family had lived in them since 1887. My great-granddad was the Gate Keeper and subsequent generations of my family lived in the cottage until 1965.

When I started working for the City Council in 2003, I was surprised to learn the cottages were owned by them, used as admin offices for one of the children's homes. As I was working in the Children and Families department, I was very keen to visit them.

My boss was very accommodating and we went in search of my family home's history. It was lovely to look over the cottages and I took my Aunty Margaret, who also grew up in the cottages.

Every time my boss now visits the cottages, I say: "I hope you haven't been in my Mum's bedroom!"

Lynda Crossland, Portsmouth, Hants

We remember when...

Mick Jagger of The Rolling Stones married Bianca Perez Morena de Macias in St Tropez this week in 1971. Guests included most of the international jet set but disagreements over the number of journalists at the church meant the wedding was almost cancelled. Eight years later Mick and Bianca divorced and he married Jerry Hall in 1990. They were married for nine years.

▓ AROUND THE HOUSE ▓

When you only need a drop or two of lemon juice don't cut it in half but pierce the rind with a clean knitting needle and squeeze out what you need.

▓ TOP TIP ▓

To avoid ants coming indoors, find the ants' entry point and sprinkle dried mint or red pepper at the spot, which seems to do the trick.

Mrs L Mandis, Degenham, Essex

Great gardening

Physocarpus

A native of North America, the shrub physocarpus only recently appeared in UK gardens. Although Physocarpus opulifolius 'Diabolo' and 'Dart's Gold' have both proved popular, the newest variety 'Lady in Red' is bound to be even more well-received. Compact in size, making it suitable for smaller gardens, its leaves are an amazingly vibrant colour. It's unusual for Hardy's Cottage Garden Plants to show a shrub at the RHS Chelsea Flower Show but the nursery owners thought it combined so well with their herbaceous perennials, they included it in their catalogue.

■ To order, tel: 01256 896 533 or visit www.hardys-plants.co.uk

Superfood!

EAT MORE... ASPARAGUS

Packed with...

Dietary fibre, phosphorus, folic acid, beta-carotene, potassium and vitamins C and K.

Good for...

Stimulating the kidneys, fighting bad bacteria and keeping the bowels regular.

Get more by...

Adding 1-inch pieces to soups or keeping whole in a pasta dish. Young asparagus tips also make a great omelette filling. Boil until tender, season and add to your omelette pan just before serving.

A Grand Day Out

At 8am on Whit Monday, it was the Sunday School outing to Hunstanton. In the early post-war years money was short and holidays a rarity.

From January onwards we paid our 1/- each week and on Whit Monday a great crowd of us gathered. The three cream Cleavers coaches came slowly down Hartington Road, Leicester, everyone wanting to get on the newest one, the teenagers claiming the back seats.

After various travel sickness and refreshments stops, we looked for the first sign of the sea.

Finally we arrived, all of us heading for the beach. Some families did their own thing, while others gathered on the sand for competitions and games.

There were visits to the amusement arcade, the fairground and shops. Tea had been arranged at the Pavilion Café – sandwiches, cakes, jellies and ice-creams.

After there was just time for a last quick paddle, when disaster struck! The ground shifted beneath my feet and down I went, soaked to the skin. To my dismay, I had to wear a pair of baggy shorts and a ladies cardigan tucked up round me. As I boarded the coach I didn't want anyone to see me, especially one young lady with large brown eyes and light olive skin with whom I imagined myself in love.

Names were read out,

Trevor – on board a bus, of course!

numbers double-checked and home again, to the singing of Ten Green Bottles and One Man Went To Mow.

No-one was sick on the way home and the hat was passed round for the driver – it had been a grand day out.

**Trevor Pheasey,
Woodford Halse, Northants**

Great gardening

Roses

The rose has been voted our favourite plant on many occasions and there are now hundreds of spectacular varieties to choose between. Although we tend to plant them centre stage – and most warrant such a place in our gardens – there are many that also do well in the background. The County series of roses makes great groundcover, producing small bushy plants (around 30cm in height) that are covered in blooms all summer. One of the most recent releases is the variety 'County of Hampshire' which has masses of light pink, slightly scented flowers.

■ It's available from Notcutts Garden Centres - visit www.notcutts.co.uk

A Grand Day Out

In May 1995, my dearly loved late mother, Kate Peachey, was invited to the 100th Sunday School Anniversary of Carmarthen Road Church, Swansea, where she been brought up, and I was very proud to accompany her.

She was wearing the light grey jacket she was particularly fond of. Although I gave all her clothes to charity when she died in 2000, I couldn't bring myself to part with the jacket, so it's comforting to see it hanging in our hall

Phyllis Roberts, Swansea

Left: Phyllis and her dear mother Kate

AROUND THE HOUSE

If you're looking for furnishings for your newly decorated room, paint a piece of white cardboard with your colour scheme, to use as a guide. When you find a material you like, ask to take a sample swatch home, and see what it looks like in various lights.

Superfood!

EAT MORE... RASPBERRIES

Packed with...

Vitamins B3 and C, potassium, magnesium, calcium and phosphorus.

Good for...

Helping to expel toxins from the body, such as mucus and phlegm.

Get more by...

Making a rich berry smoothie. Blend up raspberries with a handful of blackcurrant and blueberries and a dollop of yoghurt.

In the kitchen

THAI STIRFRY

Serves 2

- 225 g (8 oz) lean beef, lamb or pork steaks, cut into thin strips
- 5 ml (1 teaspoon) oil
- 2 cloves garlic, crushed
- 2 cm (1in) root ginger
- 1 red or green chilli, deseeded and chopped
- 50 g (2 oz) mushrooms, chopped
- 4 spring onions, chopped
- 10 ml (1 dessertspoon) fish sauce
- 15 ml (1 tablespoon) lemon juice
- 5 ml (1 teaspoon) soy sauce
- 15 ml (1 tablespoon) peanut butter – optional

1 In a large non-stick wok or saucepan, fry the meat in the oil until browned.

2 Add the garlic, ginger and chilli for 1-2 minutes. (Alternatively use 1-2 teaspoons of Thai curry paste and leave out sauce ingredients.)

3 Add remaining ingredients and cook for 2-3 minutes.

4 Serve with boiled rice noodles and stirfry vegetables.

Recipe courtesy www.meatmatters.com

We remember when...

A terrifying tornado swept through the south of England this week in 1950, causing massive damage in London, Buckinghamshire and Cambridgeshire. The tornado was so strong that it lifted parked cars, cattle and horses, and uprooted hundreds of trees. It lasted for two and a half hours and left devastation in its wake.

My childhood home

1 Woolverns Cottages

Paradise? To me, aged eight, yes. To my mother, probably not. In coronation year my family – mum, dad, sister and brother – moved from a grotty mansion flat in South Norwood to a farm cottage in Hatchford, outside Cobham, Surrey.

No 1, Woolverns Cottage, was one of a pair of back-to-back cottages which stood at the end of a dirt lane running through bluebell woods.

There was no electricity, gas, running water, bathroom or toilet. We had to pump our water from a well in the garden and used Tilley paraffin lamps for light.

In the spring we picked daffodils, cowslips and primroses from the bank of the River Mole, and we spent hours playing in the woods nearby, making dens in the rhododendron bushes. During the summer holidays we spent hours exploring Chatley Heath, armed with bottles of drink and sandwiches.

For play on more dismal days, my sister and I filled empty food cartons, jars, tins and packets with sand and set up 'shop' in the big shed.

I have so many memories of living in the cottage; mum sitting on the front step shelling peas; whiling away warm summer evenings on the wooden garden seat which dad had made; having to go with my sister, torch in hand, to the outside toilet on dark evenings.

Just before my 12th birthday, the farmer gave us notice to quit as he needed the cottage for a farm worker, and eventually we were offered temporary accommodation in an ex-army hut on the Gunsite in Cobham.

Glenys Lefouili, Worthing, W Sussex

In the kitchen

PEAR AND BLUEBERRY CAKE

- 450 g (1 lb) self-raising flour, sifted
- Pinch of salt
- 250 g (9 oz) butter, diced
- 350 g (12 oz) golden granulated sugar
- 4 large eggs, beaten
- 4 large pears, peeled, cored and sliced
- 200 g (7 oz) blueberries

1 Preheat the oven to 190°C, 375°F or Gas Mark 5. Grease and baseline a 20.5 cm (8 in) round tin.
2 Rub together the flour, salt and butter until they look like breadcrumbs. Add 250 g (9 oz) of the sugar, and the beaten egg and stir.
3 Spoon half the mix in the bottom of the tin, top with the sliced pears and the blueberries, keeping a few slices of pear and a few blueberries back. Sprinkle with the remaining sugar.
4 Spoon over the remaining cake mix. Place the remaining fruit on top pressing down slightly.
5 Bake for approximately 1 hour or until a skewer inserted in the middle comes out clean. Cool and remove from the tin. Serve warm or cold.

Recipe courtesy Billington's and Allinson

TOP TIP

A friend bought me a cotton bread bag, and it's terrific as it keeps bread fresh for so many days – great for caravan holidays.

Sophia Kramer, London N16

My childhood home

The four youngest children (Esme is on the left) when sweets had just come off ration

The Northampton house I was born in was in an old Victorian street, and had already been condemned before the Second World War. Ten of us lived in the house – Mum, Dad and eight children.

The passage was very dark, the walls varnished in brown halfway up, scratched and torn where bikes and prams had rubbed against it.

There were two bedrooms, a parlour, and a living room with stone steps going down to the kitchen. We had gas lights, no hot water, no bathroom, no heating (just a coal fire) and a lavvy at the bottom of the garden.

Every night Dad painted the bedsteads with paraffin to stop the bugs. It didn't work and when we went to bed and lifted the pillows, the bugs ran everywhere.

The house was so cold, we children argued as to whose turn it was to have the overcoats on the bed to keep warm. How Mum managed, I'll never know.

Esme Nickels MBE, Northampton

We remember when...

Petrol rationing finally came to an end on May 26, 1950. It had been rationed since 1939 but continued for more than five years after war ended. When America agreed to supply Britain with oil for petrol in return for British goods, the ban was finally lifted.

Superfood!

EAT MORE... CAULIFLOWER

Packed with...

Folate, calcium, boron, magnesium, beta-carotene, dietary fibre, potassium and vitamin C.

Good for...

Lowering blood pressure, purifying the blood and keeping bowels regular. Also thought to have anti-cancer properties and can help relieve kidney and bladder disorders.

Get more by...

Simply steaming and topping with butter-toasted breadcrumbs, basil-flavoured olive oil or chopped sun dried tomatoes in olive oil. Also delicious served raw with your favourite salsa dip.

A Grand Day Out

When I was a child my favourite day out was the Whitsun Treat. On Whit Monday, we'd all assemble in Grangetown Baptist Church, Cardiff, for a quick prayer, then at 10am we'd catch the train to Swanbridge. When the train arrived at the tiny halt, it was a long walk to Treat Field.

On the way we went along the side of the rocky beach with its island that can only be walked to at low tide. Many years before my Mother used to practise her guitar there, with the Banjo, Mandolin and Guitar Club.

When we arrived, everyone was given a currant bun and the party was on! My grandfather was always in charge of the roped-off area with the tea urns, my grandmother and the older ladies were in the large tent making sandwiches, while my father had got up early to put up the swingboats and tents.

There were races and games, then we all sat in lines on the grass with a tin cup in front of us. Trays of sandwiches were brought round and the ladies poured tea from huge enamel jugs.

After a lovely day, we'd begin to count the days until the next Whitsun Treat.

June Mead,
Wickford, Essex

AROUND THE HOUSE

Your freezer temperature should be -18°C to keep food safe. Defrost it regularly to keep it energy efficient – wrap food in newspaper when you defrost.

Great gardening
Clematis

Clematis 'Bourbon' is one of the latest cultivars to be bred by Raymond Evison at his famous nursery on Guernsey. Producing an abundance of flowers from both old and new growth between late May and September, its vibrant red petals are offset by a lovely twirl of yellow anthers. Try growing it through other wall-trained shrubs – you'll find its flowers associate well with gold or silver variegated foliage. They also complement blue, cream or yellow-flowered plants, so look wonderful with ceanothus and stunning with Cytisus battandieri. It reaches 1.8m in height, but should only be lightly pruned in March, when any dead, weak or spindly growth should be removed.

■ www.guernsey-clematis.com

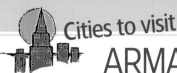
ARMAGH: ANCIENT AND MODERN

St Patrick's domain

Believed to be one of the oldest towns in Ireland, Armagh is most famous for its association with Saint Patrick. The hillside city has two cathedrals that bear the name of the country's patron saint but the county town's name is even older than Christianity – the name Armagh derives from Ard Macha and refers to a legendary pagan queen called Macha who built a fortress there.

Armagh's elegant Georgian architecture includes one of its most distinctive buildings, the County Museum which has a wide variety of exhibits as well as an impressive art collection by well-known Irish artists. Another distinctive building is the Observatory on College Hill. Also on College Hill is the Planetarium where visitors can book to see brilliant depictions of the night sky. Nearby is the city's most famous open space, The Mall. Originally created in 1773, The Mall has recently won a civic award for its restoration.

Another pleasant stroll is in the grounds of the Primate's Palace, formerly the home of the

Archbishop of the Church of Ireland. Visitors to the Palace Stables Heritage Centre can see how the stables operated in 1786 as well as looking round the Georgian kitchen and the walled kitchen garden.

In the centre of the city is the Market Place Theatre and Arts Centre.

May is the perfect month to visit Armagh when the surrounding countryside is a sea of apple blossom. St Patrick is said to have planted the first apple tree 3,000 years ago and today the county's orchards grow Bramley apples to export worldwide.

Our village

Tennis at the vicarage
Peg Southam of Poole in Dorset was never bored in the country

At the age of eight I came from a bustling city in South Wales to a village on the borders of Herefordshire and Shropshire. My grandparents brought me up and our house was a two-up, two-down black and white Tudor cottage with two acres of orchard and garden. Here we grew plums, damsons, pears, apples and all the soft fruits except redcurrants. We kept a goat which provided us with milk and cottage cheese which grandma made by shaking the milk in a big jar for hours.

The village boasted a church and a school, two pubs, a post office, baker, butcher and two general stores which between them sold everything we needed. Just as well, because only the vicar and the gentry owned cars. Transport to our nearest towns, Leominster and Ludlow, was provided by 'shopping buses' on two days a week. These were real social occasions for the local ladies who climbed aboard laden with baskets of eggs and produce for the market. It was a wonderful chance to exchange all the news and scandal.

Despite the lack of books (I was an avid reader but there was no library nearby) I was never bored. There was our Girl Guide company and I was in the church choir. We watched horses being shoed at the smithy, played Pooh sticks in the Millbrook and tennis at the vicarage.

Once a year, a concert party would arrive at the village hall. The party comprised just a small family who did everything – singing, dancing and comedy. The farm labourers had little money to spare for 'that load of nonsense' but we girls loved the matinee with a competition for the best 'turn'. I was so puffed up when I won a propelling pencil for my tap dance!

PIC: REX FEATURES

Sexy Seventies

1 In which year did the Space Hopper first appear in Britain?
A 1970
B 1971
C 1972
D 1974

2 Who was the British Foreign Secretary from 1970-1974?
A Alec Douglas Home
B Reginald Maudling
C Roy Jenkins
D Anthony Barber

3 In Starsky & Hutch, what was the make and model of Starsky's car?
A Ford Mustang
B Cheverolet Camaro
C Pontiac Firebird
D Ford Gran Torino

4 What is David Bowie's (right) real name?
A David Jones
B Tony Visconti
C David Smith
D Mick Ronson

5 How many world records did Sebastian Coe break in 1979?
A 1
B 2
C 3
D 4

6 The 1971 classic, Dirty Harry starred Clint Eastwood. Who was originally offered the title role?
A Robert Redford
B Frank Sinatra
C Sean Connery
D George Segal

7 Red Rum won the Grand National in 1977. Was this the famous horse's…?
A First win
B Second win
C Third win
D Forth win

8 What was the Christmas number one single in 1973?
A Merry Xmas Everybody – Slade
B Lonely This Christmas – Mud
C Mull of Kintyre – Wings
D When A Child Is Born – Johnny Mathis

9 Brazil won the 1970 World Cup. Who did they defeat in the final?
A Germany
B Italy
C France
D Belgium

10 What was the name of Dennis Waterman's character in The Sweeney?
A George Carter
B Jack Reagan
C George Reagan
D Frank Carter

Answers: 1 B, 2 A, 3 D, 4 A, 5 C, 6 B, 7 C, 8 A, 9 B, 10 A

Clay in his hands

Margaret Walker may have been good at maths and English at school but please don't get her started on crafts...

I try to cross the road near the school but it's nearly half past three and the procession of 'people carriers' has begun. It wasn't like this in my day. Yes, I know that phrase immediately brands me as being old, but when I was a little girl everyone walked to school.

Back then, having been crossed the road, I walked to my infants' school via the allotments, where fathers grew potatoes and carrots as part of their war effort. As I drew nearer I reached for my hanky to ward off the evil stench of boiling gluttonous bones coming from the tannery and glue works opposite school.

Their pungent smells combined with the chalk dust, stale school dinners and rancid milk, which clung to the rim of the little milk bottles from which we drank at playtime.

'Jefferson, Fairbrother, Watson, Jackson...'

'Present, Miss Taylor' we chanted in our infants' singsong. We sat at double desks in four rows: top girl and top boy at the back left, row one, then in order right through to bottom girl and bottom boy at the front of row four; the class, the happy hunting ground for Nitty Nora, the 'Hair Explorer'.

I sat next to a pale, gawky boy with horn-rimmed glasses. He shared honours with me in arithmetic and English and I didn't like him. His mother made him play piano duets with me at the Sunday School parties. His only virtue was that he was equally as bad as I was at craft.

When Beacon Reader book two and arithmetic slates had given way to the craft lesson, row four rejoiced. For the two of us on the 'top desk' it was torture. Which

Which was the least of the three evils? Knitting, raffia or clay?

was the least of the three evils? Knitting, raffia or clay? Definitely knitting. My mother had taught me to knit when I was four, to keep me quiet during British and Foreign Bible Society meetings. I'd already mastered dolls' scarves with stripes.

Row one, however, was given raffia work. Wouldn't you have thought there might have been a raffia shortage in the war? No such luck. I was armed with a bendy disc of khaki cardboard with a circle cut in the middle.

Around this I had to wind and buttonhole yards of purple raffia to make a tablemat. By week one I'd managed to splinter my raffia into straggly strands, and by week two had got the whole thing into such a mess that I prodded it feverishly with my needle, producing irretrievable knots.

Miss Taylor wasn't impressed and held it up at the end of the lesson to show Class 3 how not to make a mat. Tears of mortification welled up in my

Margaret aged 6, in 1946 – round about raffia-burning age!

eyes, and I started to plan the mat's demise.

Instead of putting it into the craft bag hanging from the teacher's desk, I hid it down my navy knickers until, in the secrecy of the allotments, I took out the offending scratchy article and ran home.

The fire was burning brightly in the black Yorkist range, where the old sooty kettle was puffing and spurting in anticipation of tea. The mat went up in a flurry of yellow and green hissing flames in a satisfying cremation.

Next week's craft lesson, and, 'Margaret Jefferson, where is your mat?' 'I don't know, Miss Taylor,' I lied. Ashes to ashes and dust to dust would have been the

The mat went up in a flurry of yellow and green hissing flames

honorable answer.

'Well, for this week you'll have to get on with something else. (Please God, let it be knitting.) 'You can do clay,' said Miss Taylor. God was having his revenge.

Even worse than that knotty, splitting raffia was the thought of putting my hands into horrid cold, wet clay. I hated it then. I hate it now. Clay at infants' school, clay on my father's allotment, and clay in our first vicarage garden. Slimy yellow ochre when wet; hard, unyielding lumps when dry…

The tutor at the senior citizens' Art Club suggests that I have a break from painting and try pottery – clay modelling is such fun. I recoil. I mean, if your raffia mat's a flop you can always burn it, but what do you do with a failed pot? Put it on the fire and its deformity is preserved forever. I decline the clay class.

My grandson was four last week…

'Grandma, can you help me with my bowl?' Oh no, it's clay!

'It's messy,' he says. I sympathise but cannot bear the thought of his lop-sided bowl being held up by the Miss Taylor of his infants' class in his first term. I weaken, and borrow my daughter's yellow rubber gloves and get stuck in. Clay in my grandson's hands.

June 2008

Sunday

I

Monday

2   Anniversary of Elizabeth II's coronation

Tuesday

3   Yours magazine on sale

Wednesday

4

Thursday

5

Friday

6

Saturday

7   The Derby, Epsom

Sunday

8

Monday

9

Tuesday

IO

Wednesday

II   Pentecost (Whitsun)

Thursday

I2

Friday

I3

Saturday

I4

Sunday

I5   Fathers' Day

Monday

I6

Tuesday

I7   Yours magazine on sale

Wednesday

I8

Thursday

I9

Friday

20   Summer Solstice

Saturday

2I

Sunday

22

Monday

23 Wimbledon Lawn Tennis Championship begins

Tuesday

24

Wednesday

25

Thursday

26

Friday

27

Saturday

28

Sunday

29

Monday

30

PIC: REX FEATURES

Born this month

Popular performer Bob Monkhouse was born in Beckenham, Kent on June 1, 1928. Best known for presenting For Love or Money and Family Fortunes, his career spanned four decades, until his death in 2003.

Married this month

Hollywood icon Marilyn Monroe (pictured) surprised the world by marrying literary playwright Arthur Miller on June 29, 1956. He had divorced his wife, Mary, to marry the legend, but he and Marilyn divorced five years later.

Died this month

Showbiz veteran Fred Astaire died on June 22, 1987, from pneumonia, in Los Angeles, California. His stage and film career had spanned 76 years!

In the kitchen

MEATY MANGO KEBABS WITH SPICED COUS COUS

Serves 2 – 4

- 450 g (1 lb) lean beef, lamb or pork cubes, cubed
- 30 ml (2 tablespoons) mango chutney
- 1 red onion, chopped
- 5 ml (1 teaspoon) oil
- 1 courgette, cut into chunks
- 50 g (2 oz) sultanas
- 15 ml (1 tablespoon) curry paste
- 300 ml (1/2 pt) meat stock
- 110 g (4 oz) cous cous
- 2 tomatoes, chopped

1 Thread the beef, lamb or pork cubes on to skewers. Cook under a pre-heated grill for approximately 4 minutes each side, until cooked through. Then brush the kebabs with the mango chutney and grill for 1-2 minutes. Turn kebabs and repeat.

2 Meanwhile, in a saucepan gently fry the red onion in the oil for 2-3 minutes. Add the courgette and cook for a further minute.

3 Add the sultanas, curry paste and meat stock. Bring to the boil. Turn off the heat, stir through the cous cous and tomatoes.

4 Cover and leave for approximately 5 minutes until all the liquid is absorbed.

Recipe courtesy www.meatmatters.com

TOP TIP

When you're having difficulty solving anagrams, use Scrabble pieces and you'll solve them in no time. If you don't have a set, write the word out in big letters and cut them up.

Sheila Waite, Torquay, Devon

AROUND THE HOUSE

If you're machining in a zip, try sticky-taping it into position. You can then stitch through it and remove the tape afterwards.

A Grand Day Out

Helen on the Great Wall of China

We were touring China in 1989, just after the student uprising in Beijing's Tiananmen Square on June 5, demanding democratic rights and ignoring the government's warnings of severe punishment.

We felt like ambassadors for democracy as we stood in the square, trying to imagine what it must have been like to see a column of tanks approaching.

According to legend, 'Nobody can be a true hero' unless they have travelled along the Great Wall of China. We tourists puffed our way up the steep incline and, nearing the last few steps, I put my hands at the back of my knees and dragged my legs in turn to reach my goal.

Memories of my grand day out at the Great Wall will remain strong but so too will the insights into the people and their culture which are so different from our own.   **Helen Gibb, Penicuik, Midlothian**

We remember when...

Twenty-five year old Queen Elizabeth II took her coronation oath this week in 1953.

She was then crowned at a coronation ceremony in Westminster Abbey in London and then left for Buckingham Palace in the golden State Coach, cheered by millions of people.

Street parties were held throughout the UK and more than 20 million people watched the event on televisions, many newly bought for the occasion.

Superfood!

Packed with...

Calcium, zinc, potassium, ribloflavin and vitamins B2, B12 and D. Also contains high amounts of 'friendly' live bacteria.

Good for...

The gut and can help prevent yeast and urinary tract infections. A great bone and teeth booster too.

Get more by...

Spooning on to breakfast cereal or mixing with dried fruit, such as prunes, figs and apple rings. Also makes a great addition to any smoothie.

Great gardening

Hibiscus syriacus

Producing spectacular flowers all summer long, varieties of Hibiscus syriacus have won many gardening fans. Although part of the mallow family, they hail from warmer parts of the globe than the annual mallows and lavateras we enjoy here. Nevertheless, H syriacus will thrive if given a sunny position and well-drained soil. Notcutts specialises in hibiscus and its newest release, Hibiscus syriacus 'Shintaeyang', looks like being another winner. Producing large, white, single flowers with a scarlet, rayed eye between July and October, it's a lovely plant to place in the centre of sunny border. Reaching around 1.8m in height, it's available from Notcutts Garden Centres, www.notcutts.co.uk for more details.

My childhood home

Ivy Cottage was the first home I remember – 58 Epping New Road, Buckhurst Hill, Essex. A small square two-storey brick house, situated on the edge of a large construction yard where my father worked. My parents moved into it in 1928, renting the cottage from French's during the 17 years Dad worked for W & C French Ltd.

We had a kitchen with a gas stove and a spacious bathroom upstairs, a dining room, drawing room and two bedrooms had their own fireplaces.

My little home had a tiny front garden and an even tinier back yard. My mother kept the front garden attractive with Irises, Lupins and daffodils, and down the far side ran a long rose arbour, a picture for most of the summer.

The gate in the back fence led directly into the yard, and the ramshackle smithy. I spent hours watching old Tong the blacksmith, fit horseshoes to the giant Clydesdale workhorses. During working hours I was not allowed in the yard, which was filled with lorries, bulldozers, self-propelled cranes and earth movers, but at weekends it became my playground.

Ivy Cottage didn't suffer a great deal from the Blitz, although one Christmas – perhaps from being shaken up a bit during air raids – the chimneypot fell into the backyard, only minutes after I'd gone inside from playing right where it fell. But ours was a sturdy little cottage and held many happy memories for me during my childhood, up to late 1947.

**M Denman Lalonde,
British Columbia**

Above: Ivy Cottage in the 1930s, and, Left: in 1983

We remember when...

Conservative minister Margaret Thatcher (later Prime Minister) planned to end free school milk for children over the age of seven this week in 1971, arguing that it would free up money to spend on other areas of education. Milk was first introduced into schools in 1924 to protect children against malnutrition and Mrs Thatcher's idea was universally unpopular.

■ AROUND THE HOUSE

If you're going away on holiday, remember to put your name and address inside your suitcase. And mark your case with something bright, such as coloured tape or ribbon, so you can recognise it easily on the airport carousel.

■ TOP TIP

One of the feet on my footstool came adrift and it wouldn't screw back into the hole. I surrounded the screw with sticky tack and screwed it back in. Perfect!

Mrs J Wisdom, Dartford, Kent

A Grand Day Out

Maisie (the littlest one) and her family waiting for a tow home

Looking back, I don't suppose our family days out were particularly grand but I, being the youngest, certainly thought they were.

My dad had a small car and when he could spare the time from his land – usually a Sunday – the family piled in, sitting on each other's laps to make room. (I would never go without a handbag, one of my mother's old ones.)

We set off towards Albury in Surrey which was where my mother had lived as a child. Sometimes we had a picnic at Newlands Corner – that is, if we got that far!

The car had a habit of breaking down, either on the way there, or back and then we would have to wait on the side of the road until someone came to tow us home.

I didn't mind because there were always flowers to pick or daisy chains to make. My mother eventually refused to go out on our jaunts; my sisters found other things to do, and my brother had always declined, preferring to stay with his mates. When the war came, trips were out.

But I still have the snapshot and, grand or not, they were happy days.

Maisie Dance, Purley, Surrey

In the kitchen

■ UPSIDE-DOWN RHUBARB AND GINGER CAKE

- 50 g (2 oz) butter
- 200 g (7 oz) light muscovado sugar
- 350 g (12 oz) fresh rhubarb, trimmed and cut into 2 cm (1 in) pieces
- 2 tablespoons finely chopped stem ginger
- 200 g (7 oz) plain flour
- 1 teaspoon baking powder
- 1/4 teaspoon bicarbonate of soda
- 1/2 teaspoon salt
- Finely grated zest of 1 orange
- 200 ml (approx 7 fl oz) buttermilk
- 2 medium eggs
- 80 ml (approx 3 fl oz) vegetable oil

1 Preheat the oven to 180°C, 350°F or Gas Mark 4.

2 Melt the butter in a 24cm (9¹/₂in) ovenproof frying pan over a medium heat. Stir in half the sugar, and cook for about 5 minutes. Remove from the heat and add the rhubarb and ginger.

3 If you don't have an ovenproof frying pan, pour the rhubarb mix into a 24 cm (9¹/₂ in) round tin.

4 Mix together the flour, baking powder, bicarbonate of soda, salt and orange zest.

5 Whisk the remaining sugar with the buttermilk, eggs and oil. Add the flour mix and mix well. Pour over the rhubarb and smooth the surface.

6 Bake for 30 minutes or until the cake springs back when pressed in the centre. Cool, then invert on to a serving plate. Serve warm with custard or cream.

Recipe courtesy Billington's and Allinson

Great gardening

Kaleidoscope

The gardening world has been struggling to create a stable, variegated, compact abelia for many years. Now it has, thanks to the American Randy Lindsey of Panoramic Farm. 'Kaleidoscope' has lovely flowers and a dense growth habit, but its real attraction is its dynamic colours. Changing from a wonderful gold margin in spring, the leaves intensify during the summer until they turn red, orange and yellow in autumn. 'Kaleidoscope' thrives in moist, well-drained, acidic soil and colours best when planted in full sun. It reaches 90cm in height and is available from Notcutts Garden Centres, or www.notcutts.co.uk

Superfood!

EAT MORE... PEPPERS

Packed with...

Vitamins B6, B1, E, A, K and C, fibre, manganese, folate, copper, tryptophan, potassium and beta carotene.

Good for...

Helping to lower high cholesterol levels and blood pressure, preventing cancers of the cervix, bladder and pancreas, boosting the secretion of stomach acid and saliva and protecting against cataracts.

Get more by...

Serving in a crudite platter, stuffing with your favourite rice salad and baking until tender or finely chopping into any leaf-based salad.

My childhood home

Number 39 Stanton Street, Peckham was the home of the Pays family – six boys and two girls. My mother, Flo, organised the street party for King George and Queen Elizabeth's coronation in 1937, complete with flags, food and cake.

Ours was a happy house that backed on to the Surrey canal – we had a deep (and spooky) coal cellar.

In those days betting was illegal. When a bookie's runner was being chased by the police, my Mum would open the street door, and he would run through the house, throwing his bag down the cellar, then he'd run out the back and over the fence and the police would lose him over the canal bridge. It still makes me smile.

Dorothy Snaith, London SE26

Bottom, right: Dorothy in the back garden
Bottom, left: No 39 Stanton Street
Below: Dorothy's Mum, Flo (right)
at the coronation party in 1937

Great gardening

Lavender

L avender has been hugely popular in this country for many years, as it's a valuable addition to cooking, when creating perfume, and in medicine. It comes from the Mediterranean, where it enjoys well-drained soils and plenty of sun. However, if you give it the right conditions, it will thrive in our gardens as well. Lavandula angustifolia 'Elizabeth' is one of the newest varieties and produces large fragrant spikes of dark purple flowers above grey leaves.

■ Plants can be ordered from Downderry Nursery, tel: 01732 810 081 or visit www.downderry-nursery.co.uk

A Grand Day Out

Dorothea (second right) on her Midsummer picnic

E very Midsummer's day Stratford Writers' Study Group has a riverside picnic beside the Avon. We arrive in cars loaded with food, drink and picnic seats, and cross the river by ferry.

On the other side we find a shady spot under a willow tree and settle ourselves for the afternoon.

We then make short work of the food – ham sandwiches, sausage rolls, cheese straws, and cherries, strawberries and cream

We finish with readings from Wind in the Willows and Three Men in a Boat. Strangely, we always have good weather!

Dorothea Abbott, Stratford-upon-Avon

We remember when...

Princess Diana gave birth to her first son, William, on June 21, 1982, at St Mary's Hospital in London. William weighed 7lb 1 1/2 oz and was the first heir to the British throne to be born in a hospital. Crowds gathered outside the hospital and Buckingham Palace awaiting news of the birth. The prince was formally named William Arthur Philip Louis Mountbatten Windsor.

Superfood!

EAT MORE... AUBERGINES

Packed with...

Vitamin C and A, calcium, beta-carotene, magnesium, potassium and phosphorous.

Good for...

Protecting arteries, cleaning the blood and preventing strokes.

Get more by...

Stuffing with walnuts, chopped onions, tomatoes and garlic and topping with grated cheese. Bake for 25 to 35 minutes on a medium heat.

In the kitchen

■ BROAD BEAN, GRUYÈRE AND BACON OMELETTE

Serves 4

- ■ 250 g (9 oz) podded broad beans
- ■ 150 g (5 oz) good quality streaky bacon rashers, diced
- ■ 6 eggs
- ■ 75 g (3 oz) Gruyère cheese, grated
- ■ 15 g butter (½ oz)
- ■ Salt and pepper

1 Cook the broad beans in boiling water for 4-5 minutes. Drain and rinse under cold water. Shell the beans and discard the skins if necessary but very small, young beans will be fine as they are.

2 Heat a frying pan and dry-fry the bacon until cooked through and beginning to brown. Remove the bacon and wipe the pan out with paper towels to get rid of any excess fat.

3 In a bowl, lightly beat the eggs and add two thirds of the cheese, and season.

4 Melt the butter in the frying pan and add the beans and bacon, followed by the egg and cheese mixture. Stir gently with a fork to combine, then leave to cook over a very low heat until set but still a little runny on top.

5 Heat the grill. Sprinkle the remaining cheese over the omelette and grill until the top has set.

6 Serve the omelette warm or at room temperature, cut into wedges, accompanied by a crisp salad.

Recipe courtesy The English Pea & Bean Season

My childhood home

I was born in Bristol in 1949, where my parents had a pet stores and garden shop in Gloucester Road – we sold budgies, canaries and tortoises.

From the shop, there was a small hallway which led into the kitchen cum dining room which overlooked the garden. From one of our windows we had a plank going down to the garden so they could go in and out. We lived in this room most of the time and had a coal fire going all day during the winter months.

Off the landing were three doors, one of which went into the sitting room, which was only used on Sundays, high days and holidays. Sundays were special

and my mother would sit at the piano and play hymns and other music, so we could sing along.

I slept with my two sisters in the back bedroom, which was through the bathroom.

To get to the long garden, we had to go through the shop and down some very steep stairs into the basement, where there were four storerooms. One of these was our playroom which led into the garden. We had a special little garden for our Welsh corgi, Jane.

When we were older and had forgotten our house keys,

Below: Elizabeth with her corgi, Jane
Left: Elizabeth's childhood home

we would ring the bell and Dad would open the sitting room window and throw the keys down to us, which always scared us. We were afraid he might fall out, so whoever was in the sitting room with him used to hold onto his legs, to be on the safe side.

Elizabeth Hack, Weston-super-Mare, N Somerset

In the kitchen

▮ QUICK GLAZED STRAWBERRY TARTS ▮

Makes 4

- ▪ 1 x 215 g (7 ½ oz) sheet ready-rolled puff pastry (or bought puff pastry cases)
- ▪ 30 ml (2 tablespoons) milk
- ▪ 300 ml (approx ½ pint) double cream, whipped
- ▪ 1 tablespoon Lyle's Golden Syrup
- ▪ 225 g (8 oz) strawberries, hulled and quartered
- ▪ 15 ml (1 tablespoon) Lyle's Squeezy Syrup Strawberry Flavour

1 Heat oven to 200°C, 400°F or Gas Mark 6. Lay out the puff pastry and with a 10 cm (4 in) pastry cutter, cut out 4 rounds. With a smaller 8 cm (3 in) pastry cutter, make an incision in the middle of the pastry disc, all the way through. Glaze the pastry with the milk.

2 Lay the pastry circles on a lined tray and bake in the oven for 10 mins or until risen, crisp and golden. Cool on a wire rack.

3 Very carefully cut around the inner circle (that was scored with the smaller pastry cutter) and remove. Scoop out the excess pastry from the middle to leave a crisp pastry case.

4 Mix the whipped cream and golden syrup to make a delicate, sweet Chantilly cream. Fill the cases with the cream and top with mounds of strawberries. Finally, glaze the strawberries with Lyle's Squeezy Syrup Strawberry Flavour.

Recipe courtesy Lyle's Golden Syrup

▮ TOP TIP ▮

As souvenirs of various holidays, I buy key-rings and attach them to handbags and shopping bags. It makes the zips easier to get at – and brings back a holiday memory.

Margaret Evans, Eastbourne, E Sussex

My childhood home

Margaret as a little girl

Left: Margaret's home in Crouch End

The house I grew up in was a Victorian terrace house in Crouch End, North London. I lived on the ground floor with my parents and three brothers, my uncle and granny were on the first floor, and a retired nurse and her son occupied the top floor.

We had three rooms and a scullery, which Mum used as a kitchen. I often wondered how she managed to do the cooking and washing for six people there. Dad promised he'd fit some units for her, but this never happened.

We had a long, narrow cellar which we slept in during the war. Dad even papered the walls to make it look more homely. If I came home when it was dark, I'd make a dash from the gate to the front door, as the dark steps to the cellar scared me!

The house is now converted to three flats, used for three families now, as it was years ago but now rather more sophisticated.

Margaret Brown, Colchester, Essex

We remember when...

On June 27, 1957 a report by the Medical Research Council was the first to suggest that there was a link between smoking and lung cancer. At the time tobacco companies rejected the claims but the link between smoking and lung cancer is now firmly established and on July 1, 2007, smoking indoors in public places was banned completely.

Superfood!

Packed with...

Potassium, magnesium, beta-carotene, vitamins A and C, calcium and iron.

Good for...

Maintaining healthy joints, arteries, bones and connective tissue. Also thought to have antispasmodic qualities.

Get more by...

Shredding into tacos and tortillas or adding to scrambled egg – fry a finely cut lettuce in butter for several minutes, before adding your beaten eggs, salt and pepper and scrambling together.

▮ AROUND THE HOUSE ▮

Although a certain amount of sun is good for you, as it aids the production of vitamin D, avoid exposure between 10am and 4pm during the summer months, when the sun is strongest.

Great gardening
Astilbe

One perennial most gardeners include when planting a pond, lake or stream, is the astilbe. A pretty plant, it thrives in moist conditions, whether in sun or partial shade, and reliably produces masses of summer flowers followed by attractive seedheads. The newest variety to appear in garden centres is 'Color Flash', which is so distinctive it's bound to be popular. Producing spectacular leaves of green, burgundy, red, orange and cream, it looks great even when not in flower. It's available from Notcutts Garden Centres, or visit www.notcutts.co.uk for more details.

A Grand Day Out

"If you start going to Sunday School now," my mother said, "you'll have enough stars to go on the summer outing."

So with great reluctance at having to forfeit my Sunday afternoons, I went to the Methodist Chapel. The chapel yard looked too much like the school playground for my liking and the Sunday School room wasn't much better. But after the mandatory, much-resented attendances, the big day arrived.

Transport was usually a big high-sided farm wagon drawn by two huge cart horses, our destination the local farm. We scrambled out of the cart, revelling in the feel of the soft grass.

The afternoon was spent playing games or running through the grass looking for

Eva, aged seven, all ready for her outing

birds' nests, pulling bits of lamb's wool off the fence.

Then the loud ringing of the handbell meant the sharing out of the goodies – home-made lemonade and mounds of buttered currant buns.

The return journey was always more subdued. I was never fully converted to Sunday School but, perhaps, Jesus did love me after all because I always had a good time.

Eva Coad, Leamington Spa, Warwickshire

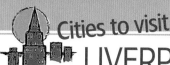

LIVERPOOL: ANCIENT AND MODERN

John, Paul and the SuperLambBanana

As European City of Culture 2008, Liverpool offers visitors an exciting range of experiences from art and music to sport. Their first port of call should be Albert Dock which has the largest collection of Grade I listed buildings in the UK as well as many inviting bars and cafés. Right on the waterfront is the port's most famous landmark and Britain's first skyscraper, The Liver Building.

Bringing the city right up to date is FACT, Liverpool's stunningly modern Centre for Film, Art & Creative Technology which has three cinemas as well as two galleries showing an international programme of film and video art.

Among the city's more unexpected tourist attractions are two subterranean venues. The Williamson Tunnels are an underground labyrinth created by a 19th century philanthropist, Joseph Williamson. The Western Approaches Museum provides an opportunity to explore the top secret underground headquarters dating from World War II.

Rivalling each other as two of Liverpool's quirkiest sights are the 15-foot high SuperLambBanana sculpture on the waterfront and the oriental Imperial Arch that spans Nelson Street – the entrance to Chinatown.

And no visit to Liverpool would be complete without enjoying a Beatles tour which includes the National Trust homes of John Lennon and Paul McCartney as well as The Cavern Club where the Swinging Sixties started.

Farmhouse teas

Rosemary Neal still lives in the Oxfordshire village where she enjoyed an idyllic childhood

Our village

On our village fête day, I met an old friend who said: "Didn't we have an absolutely wonderful childhood growing up here in Epwell?" We recalled summer holidays that always seemed sunny when we climbed the hills, taking picnics of home-made lemonade and biscuits, returning home just in time for tea.

There were lots of children in the village then, our numbers being swelled by evacuees. We roamed the lanes and fields at will. One of us had a pet gosling called Gossy who accompanied us everywhere. One day we followed the stream until we reached the mill. Gossy swam in the water ahead of us and was swept over the waterfall. We feared the worst but when we ran round to the bottom of the waterfall, we found him none the worse for his experience. We fished him out and he trotted happily along the road behind us.

Many homes were open to us. Some were those of real aunties and some were adopted aunts. On afternoons when we didn't know what to do, we would say 'let's go and see Aunt Ivy at Chillaway Farm'. She was always welcoming. Uninvited and unexpected, we were always asked to stay to tea when her table was spread with the things that children love to eat.

Rosemary, aged 9

One of the highlights of the year was the Sunday School outing. This was an expedition to the Red Barn, loaned for the occasion by the farmer. We travelled by horse and cart and, although it was only a mile and half from the village, when I was very small it seemed a long way.

Signs of the times

Mick Botting shares his love of enamelled signs, which are becoming increasingly collectable

Advertising in newspapers, on television and the internet is part of everyday life but in the days of pea soupers and ration books it was very different. Businesses relied on posters, billboards and enamelled signs to catch the eye and sell their wares.

The enamel process involved fusing a type of powdered glass to sheet metal at very high temperatures to make eye-catching and beautifully designed products in striking colours.

The world's first enamel sign factory was registered in 1889 as the Patent Enamel Company in Birmingham, and it was so successful that others followed suit.

These signs were produced until the 1950s and advertised everything from tobacco to cleaning products and confectionary .

The products often made astonishing claims – cigarettes would give you sweet-smelling breath and sex appeal!

But these signs of the past often ended up being used to make fences or improvised shed roofs. Others found their way to the rubbish tip but, having been dug up, have survived remarkably well.

Some of these signs have been reproduced

Given a good clean up, the signs are as bright and sparkly as the day they graced a shop wall 50 or 60 years ago. Others have found their way to museums and restored steam railway platforms.

Pictorial enamels are the most desirable as home decoration and it's an added bonus if the price of the product is displayed as well. Just imagine Coombs' flour in 3d packets, an 'Antidote for Indigestion'; or Ju-vis beef tea at 1d a cup for breakfast. Cigarettes signs were painstakingly enamelled with prices such as 10 for 4d or bicycles £6-6s, or Borax

starch at 1d per packet.

Top of every collector's shopping list – if they have the money – are signs with images of Edwardian ladies, early motorcars, and animals.

Some of these signs have been reproduced but can easily be distinguished from the genuine article. They're usually much thinner metal and would probably only last a few months out in the elements. They're even given rust holes and scratches to try to make them look authentic.

There's a dedicated band of collectors that subscribe to the Street Jewellery Review magazine to exchange news, swap, buy and sell signs.

So if you see an enamel sign at a boot sale or in an antique shop going for a few pounds, snap it up quickly! You can be sure you'll have made a killing, and it could take pride of place in your modern-day kitchen.

◆ Secretary of Street Jewellery Review is Andrew Morley. Visit www.streetjewellery.org or email Andrew for more details: info@streetjewellery.org

July 2008

Tuesday

1
Yours magazine on sale

Wednesday

2
Henley Royal Regatta begins

Thursday

3

Friday

4
American Independence Day

Saturday

5

Sunday

6

Monday

7

Tuesday

8

Wednesday

9

Thursday

10

Friday

11

Saturday

12

Sunday

13

Monday

14
Battle of the Boyne (Bank Holiday N. Ireland)

Tuesday

15
St. Swithun's Day
Yours magazine on sale

Wednesday

16

Thursday

17

Friday

18

Saturday

19

Sunday

20

Monday

21

Tuesday

22

Wednesday

23
....

Thursday

24
....

Friday

25
....

Saturday

26
....

Sunday

27
....

Monday

28
....

Tuesday

29
....

Wednesday

30
....

Thursday

31
....

PIC: REX FEATURES

Born this month

British actress Diana Rigg (pictured) was born on July 20, 1938 in Doncaster. Best known for her roles as Emma Peel in The Avengers and as James Bond's wife in the film On Her Majesty's Secret Service.

Married this month

Prince Charles married Lady Diana Spencer on July 29, 1981 at St Paul's Cathedral, London. It's thought 750 million people around the world watched the wedding on television.

Died this month

Academy award-winning British actor David Niven died of Motor Neurone disease at the age of 73, on July 29, 1983. He starred in almost 100 films throughout his career.

My childhood home

My Father was very badly injured in the First World War but he came home, and in 1918 married my Mother. A year later they came to live in this house; my late sister and I were both born at home, in 1921 and 1928 respectively.

Once, the house was full with my grandmother, Mother, Father and sister, and during the Second World War my Mother had evacuees here from Margate – their name was Saffery, and I often wonder about them.

I have lived here all my life, with the large garden which was always full of vegetables, the old tumbledown pigsty – we kept a pig and chickens – and the outside privy which is still up the top of the garden. When it snowed, we had to dig a pathway to get to it.

The house is 200 years old, but it has had a 'makeover' to modernise it, so here I sit with my two darling cats and my memories.

Top: Minnie's house
Above: The pigsty and privy end

Minnie Wade, Rugeley, Staffs

▌AROUND THE HOUSE▐

Save water! Remember to turn off the tap while you're cleaning your teeth, as leaving it on can waste 2 gallons of water.

Great gardening

Sweet Peas

Sweet Peas are one of the easiest annual climbers to grow and, with the majority of modern varieties producing highly colourful and scented flowers all summer, it's easy to see why they're so popular. Every year the specialist nurseries release new varieties and some of the most recent introductions include 'Banty' (rose pink flowers and an Award of Garden Merit from the RHS), 'Colleen Mary' (with salmon and cream-coloured flowers) and 'Misty' (with mauve flushed petals).

■ All three are available from Eagle Sweet Peas and seeds can be ordered, tel: 01889 270 215 or visit www.eaglesweetpeas.co.uk.

Superfood!

▌EAT MORE... FENNEL▐

Packed with...

Calcium, magnesium, potassium, phosphorus, phyto-oestrogens, iron and vitamin C.

Good for...

Relieving stomach pains and cramps, as it has antispasmodic properties. Also thought to help the digestion of fat, so may be useful for weight control.

Get more by...

Braising, grilling, stewing or adding to mashed potato. Also delicious raw – add to coleslaws and salads or slice and dip into extra virgin olive oil seasoned with ground black pepper.

In the kitchen

▦ THYME-SCENTED COURGETTE COUS COUS ▦

Serves 6

- Small pinch saffron strands
- 225 g (8 oz) cous cous
- 15g (approx ¹/₂ oz) butter for greasing
- 1 tablespoon fresh thyme leaves
- Salt and coarsely ground black pepper
- 90 ml (6 tablespoons)olive oil
- 30 ml (2 tablespoons) lemon juice
- 5 ml (1 teaspoon) Dijon mustard
- 225 g (8 oz) courgettes, coarsely grated
- 1 bunch spring onions, finely chopped
- Salt and pepper

1 Preheat the oven to 200°C, 400°F or Gas Mark 6. Pour 150 ml (¹/₄ pint) boiling water over the saffron strands and set aside for 5 minutes.

2 Put the cous cous in a small, lightly buttered, ovenproof dish and stir in the saffron liquid with enough extra cold water to come level with the top of the grains. Leave to swell for 5 minutes.

3 Stir in the thyme leaves and season with salt and pepper. Cover the dish with buttered foil and bake in the oven for 20 minutes.

4 While the cous cous is baking, whisk together the olive oil, lemon juice and mustard, then stir the dressing into the grated courgettes and spring onions. Leave to marinate.

5. When the cous cous is hot, stir in the courgette mixture and serve immediately.

Recipe courtesy www.thinkvegetables.co.uk

We remember when...

All food rationing ended on July 4, 1954, as restrictions on meat and bacon were lifted. Altogether there had been 14 years of shortages; queueing outside shops and bartering for extra food had become part of daily life. Everything from food to clothes, soap, furniture and fuel were rationed. De-rationing began in 1948.

A Grand Day Out

Gwen (second right) and her family on their holidays

My Mother's sister and her family lived in Moordown, Bournemouth and my parents, brother, sister and I spent many of our summer holidays with them in the 1920s.

We'd set out from Wales at 5.30am in my Dad's Bullnose Morris with its folding roof, celluloid side curtains and can of Pratt's petrol (one shilling and ninepence a gallon) strapped on the running board.

We saw lovely sunrises and would see maids cleaning the steps of large houses – my Dad would shout, 'Good morning' and when they waved back we would giggle. We'd arrive about 4pm – no Severn Bridge in those days, only the Aust ferry which my mother didn't like.

The next morning my cousins and three of us would go to a cake shop to buy six pennyworth of stale (yesterday's) cakes and we'd take these with some sandwiches and water through Bournemouth's two lovely Pleasure Gardens to the beach, where we'd play all day on the sand, paddle in the sea and watch Punch and Judy.

I'm now in my eighties and still remember the happiness of those holidays.

May Nichols, Newport, Gwent

TOP TIP

To remove scale from chrome bath taps, soak some cotton wool in white vinegar and secure to the tap overnight for shiny clean taps.

Mrs M Bargewell, Cleveland

In the kitchen

FRUIT SMOOTHIE

Serves 2

- 110g (4oz) blueberries
- 110g (4oz) raspberries
- 110g (4oz) strawberries
- 2 tablespoons wheatgerm
- 4 tablespoons natural fat-free yoghurt
- 150ml (¼ pint) semi-skimmed milk
- Pinch light cane sugar

1 Tip all the ingredients into a blender and blend until smooth. Add more light cane sugar to taste if necessary and serve immediately over ice.

■ **Tip:** The berries may be a little sharp, so the light cane sugar sweetens the taste. Smoothies are a great alternative way of incorporating more fruit into your diet.

Recipe courtesy Tate & Lyle

Superfood!

EAT MORE... TOMATOES

Packed with...

Vitamins C, A, K, B1, B6, E and B2, potassium, manganese, fibre, chromium, folate, copper, iron, magnesium and beta carotene.

Good for...

Reducing the risk of cardiovascular disease and some cancers. Also thought to prevent macular degeneration and help maintain healthy skin. A good all-round immunity booster too.

Get more by...

Making your own salsa dip by mixing with chopped onions and chilli peppers, puréeing with cucumber and peppers to make a refreshing cold soup or serving with slices of mozzarella cheese for an Italian-style salad.

Great gardening

Lily

One plant that all gardeners adore is the lily. With show-stopping blooms in wonderful colours and a great scent, it's a plant you can't ignore. New varieties appear every season and this year's no exception with the arrival of 'Souvenir', which has large pastel pink blooms with a white centre. It's extremely fragrant but only reaches 35cm in height, making it ideal in a container. Shelter it from strong winds and use a compost rich in organic matter.

■ It's available from Notcutts Garden Centres, visit www.notcutts.co.uk for more details.

We remember when...

Live Aid, the world's biggest rock festival, was held this week in 1985 at Wembley Stadium, London. Organised by Bob Geldof, it aimed to raise money for famine relief in Africa and made £40 million. Twenty years later, in 2005, Bob Geldof organised Live 8, a series of rock concerts worldwide to raise awareness of global poverty again before the G8 summit in Scotland in July.

AROUND THE HOUSE

Petroleum jelly will loosen stiff latches and bolts, and methylated spirit can be used to get rid of sticky marks and stubborn labels – careful, though, it's flammable.

My childhood home

The police house (on right) – Jasmine's home

My father was a local policeman at Sevenoaks in Kent, and our home was attached to the police station, so you can imagine the raised eyebrows whenever I show my birth certificate!

Part of my father's duties was to attend to any prisoners. Court day was Monday and as our yard was the only place for the prisoners to exercise, we were not allowed out that day.

The policemen were concessionary 'uncles' and many times we'd help wash the black MG patrol cars (the

Superintendent had a saloon).

When I was ten more office space was needed, so the houses were used and we moved to another police house close by. The property has now been converted into attractive apartments, and whenever I go past I have many happy childhood memories – apart from the noise of the prisoners who'd had too much alcohol!

Jasmine Jarrett, Sevenoaks, Kent

A Grand Day Out

When our son, Richard, was young he loved visiting castles and we had great days out. Imagine our delight when our granddaughter, Charlotte, who's seven, (and who lives in Singapore) told us that they'd been learning about castles at school. And could we take her to see some real castles when she comes over for her annual summer visit?

We live in Northumberland which has many famous castles, but the one Charlotte and her little brother Walter really enjoyed was Prudhoe Castle.

There was so much for them to do, including a huge book for Charlotte to read to us all, and huge

Charlotte and Walter having a great time at Prudhoe Castle

bricks with plans so they could build a castle.

There was plenty of space to explore (and not many visitors), a moat to run around, and an activity room with jigsaws, colouring in, and brass rubbings.

The children loved it, we all had a great day out and it brought back wonderful memories of the castles we visited when their father was a boy.

Barbara Cox, Hexham, Northumberland

TOP TIP

For insect bites, even mosquito bites, toothpaste from the tube will get rid of irritation and inflammation promptly.

Ralf Harland, Guildford, Surrey

We remember when...

Tesco decided to reintroduce imperial measures for weighing food in stores this week in the year 2000. European legislation had forced the change to metric weights in January, but when a survey revealed that 90 per cent of customers preferred imperial measures, Tesco found a legal loophole and now puts both versions on its packaging.

A Grand Day Out

Janet (second left) and her friend Ursula with her brother and parents at Skegness

I've recently been browsing through old photographs and mementos of my late parents, and what memories were there. Even a letter my gran sent to my Dad informing him of my birth (he was away in the Army).

When the war ended we were lucky enough to spend our annual holiday in Skegness (Dad had two sisters there) - and we used to hire a shooting brake to take us.

Mum would save tins and groceries all year round and send them in a box on the train a week before our holiday. We then used to 'keep ourselves' at Auntie's, other than getting fresh meat every day.

My parents, my brother and I would go off to the beach each day and Auntie would prepare the food for us – wonderful sunny, happy days.

Janet Thursfield, Cheadle, Staffs

In the kitchen

■ LAMB MOUSSAKA ■

Serves 4 – 6

- ■ 675 g (approx 1½ lb) lean lamb mince
- ■ 1 onion, chopped
- ■ 1 clove garlic, crushed
- ■ 45 ml (3 tablespoons) tomato purée
- ■ 30 ml (2 tablespoons) mint jelly
- ■ 2 aubergines, thinly sliced
- ■ 75 g (3 oz) feta cheese
- ■ 500 g (approx 1 lb) pot Greek yogurt
- ■ 2 eggs

1 In a non-stick pan dry fry the lamb mince for 4-5 minutes with the onion and garlic. Add tomato purée and mint jelly. Season with salt and pepper and cook for 2-3 minutes.
2 Meanwhile, lightly brown the aubergines on both sides in a hot frying pan (probably in 2 or 3 batches).
3 Place half the mince mixture into an ovenproof dish and top with some of the aubergine slices. Crumble over the feta cheese, and cover with the rest of the mince and the remaining aubergine.
4 Mix together the Greek yogurt with the eggs and pour over the aubergines. Bake in a preheated oven (180°C, 350°F, Gas Mark 4) for 30-35 minutes until golden brown.
5 Serve with a baked Greek salad – roast tomatoes, slices of red onion and olives topped with crumbled Feta cheese. Recipe courtesy www.meatmatters.com

▌TOP TIP

To keep plants watered while you're on holiday: Cut a piece of floral foam ¾in thick, to the shape of the pot holder. Soak oasis well in water, place in holder, and put the plant pot on top. Before leaving, fill pot holder with just enough water to cover oasis. It worked for my plants.

Doreen Welsh, Newton Le Willows, Merseyside

Great gardening

Summer Chocolate

The Hillier family has long been associated with horticulture and the Sir Harold Hillier Arboretum at Romsey in Hampshire, with its extensive collection of plants from all around the world, pays testament to its knowledge. However, the company is also involved in the production of new plants, of which one of the most recent is Albizia julibrissin 'Summer Chocolate'. A graceful small tree with fern-like, chocolate-coloured foliage complemented by pink, fluffy flower heads in late summer, it's bound to be popular with gardeners.

■ Order it at one of Hillier's garden centres – visit www.hillier.com

Superfood!

EAT MORE... BLUEBERRIES

Packed with...

Beta-carotene and vitamin C.

Good for...

Cleansing the blood and improving circulation, as well as benefiting eyesight and having a mild laxative effect.

Get more by...

Adding to cakes and muffins or make some delicious blueberry eggy bread – beat together 4 oz cream cheese, ¼ pint milk and a few handfuls of coarsely mashed blueberries. Add six beaten eggs and mix before dunking in your bread and frying until golden.

My childhood home

In 1928, when I was five, my family moved to my childhood home, Rosedene, in Hadleigh, Essex and I have nothing but happy memories of it.

It was opposite a small wood and a few yards further on, a very large wood, part of which is now a Nature Reserve. We had many happy times there, chestnutting, catching newts and tadpoles, picking flowers and picnicking.

It was a large bungalow in an unmade road and as it was November, the road was muddy and the removal van couldn't drive down it, so the furniture had to be carried. As I was the youngest of seven and had five older brothers, there were quite a few helpers.

There were dark corners in the

Beryl at Rosedene in about 1930

bungalow because when we first moved in, there was no electricity, and I always left the dining room door open when I went to the toilet. I also hated going to bed by candlelight in the gloom.

The front door was laid back from the rooms either side and so formed a large porch, which we used to play in on wet days.

My father grew vegetables

and every fruit imaginable in the big garden, and we had loads of corners to play hide-and-seek. In the autumn my mother made jam and pickles, a necessity with such a large family and on bonfire night we had a huge bonfire; the neighbours came round and we'd have jacket potatoes cooked in the embers.

Beryl M Kelsey, Upminster

My childhood home

Joyce's Gran by the glass lid to the shelter

The house where I was born was in Bicester Road, Richmond, Surrey, in 1939. It was a small semi with bay windows, and with a small front and back garden.

One of my earliest recollections is Dad digging a hole in the back garden, and into it building walls with a roof – our air-raid shelter. He built a rockery over the roof and the sides to disguise it. It had steps going down inside, where there were four bunks, with another emergency exit at the back.

I only remember sleeping in it once, when my brother's bunk fell on top of me, and we both got asthma, it being a rather damp environment.

After the war, Dad put a greenhouse on top of the shelter, and with the rockery down the sides, no-one knew it was there. Mum and Dad moved in the 1960s, so I expect the new owners had a surprise find!

Joyce Gale, Bristol

Great gardening
Calandiva

Many people struggle with houseplants, losing them in a matter of weeks, usually due to a chronic lack of water. If you despair of keeping your houseplants alive, then try this new plant, calandiva. A newly developed version of the popular indoor plant, kalanchoe, it's a native of Madagascar and will grow happily in sun or shade, as long as the temperature remains above 15C. Most importantly, though, it can survive infrequent watering! Ten different colours are available ranging though pale pink, cream and white to vivid magenta, red and orange – so whatever your style, there'll be a calandiva to fit the bill.

Superfood!

EAT MORE... CELERY

Packed with...

Vitamins A, B3 and C, folic acid, calcium, iron and potassium.

Good for...

Lowering blood pressure, relieving migraines and the symptoms of arthritis. Also thought to have anti-cancer properties.

Get more by...

Adding to soups and stews or filling the cavity of raw celery with soft cheeses, such as gorgonzola.

In the kitchen

▓ BRILLIANT BREAKFAST ▓

Serves 1
- 150 g (5 oz) Greek style yoghurt
- 1 tablespoon molasses sugar
- 100 g (approx 4 oz) seedless red grapes, halved if large

1 Spoon the yoghurt into a bowl and crumble over the molasses sugar. Leave for a few minutes for flavours to mingle (or longer in the fridge).
2 Sprinkle with grapes to serve.
- **Tip:** For added fibre, serve with some muesli.

Recipe courtesy Billington's

▓ AROUND THE HOUSE ▓

If you've left masking tape on too long when painting a window frame and you can't get it all off, gently scrape the bits of tape and sticky residue with a hand-held razor.

We remember when...

The space race came to a thrilling end as man walked on the moon for the first time, on July 21, 1969. As American astronaut Neil Armstrong stepped on to the moon's surface he declared: "That's one small step for man, one giant leap for mankind." Millions of people watched the moon landing live on television and it became a defining moment of the twentieth century.

An excited little girl with her Mam and Dad

I will always remember our Sunday trips to the seaside – such a big occasion and Mam would be preparing for it from Wednesday onwards.

We were lucky to have a car in 1951, and the day before our trip, Dad would polish it and I'll never forget the smell of the leather upholstery.

I could hardly sleep the night before but morning arrived at last and Mam would be in the kitchen making sandwiches – beef, ham and cheese.

Grandma and Granddad would come too on the epic journey from Doncaster to Skegness – Grandma passing the humbugs round.

I plagued Dad with, 'Are we nearly there yet?' Finally he'd announce, 'Here we are!'

I was so excited I didn't know what to do first – make a sandcastle, go for a paddle, play ball.

Dad would roll his trousers up and he and Mam would take me for a paddle; Dad would always dig a boat for me, complete with paper flags on the top.

Out would come the sandwiches and cakes and we'd finish up with ice creams. Not long after Grandma and Granddad would be snoring, still fully clothed and wearing their Sunday best hats.

Time to go home and as the car was packed, I was dried off and every grain of sand rubbed off my skin.

The next thing I remember is Dad carrying me into the house, having slept most of the way home.

**Carol Stott,
Spalding, Lincs**

We remember when...

Football history was made today as England won the World Cup this week in 1966, beating West Germany with a 4-2 victory at London's Wembley Stadium. England player Geoff Hurst became the first man ever to score a hat-trick in a World Cup final.

A Grand Day Out

Chris and her Dad
at Swallow Falls

I grew up in the late 1940s and we lived in Oakengates, Shropshire. Dad worked at a local engineering works and we looked forward to our days trips to the seaside during the factory closure at the end of July, beginning of August.

One of Dad's colleagues organised a trip to the sea – often to Wales – and the halfway stop was usually at the Swallow Falls, Betws-y-Coed. We always stopped on the return journey to drink the beer or pop stowed away in the boot of the coach.

There were two coach companies in the village, and it was with great anticipation that we waited for the destination boards to go up – Rhyl, Llandudno, Southport and New Brighton were favourites.

We also went to Shrewsbury Flower Show, the marquees were breathtaking and in the arena, showjumping, acrobats, bands and choirs. The highlight was the firework display at the end, and eating fish and chips out of newspaper on the way back to the coach.

Chris Downes, Telford, Shrops

In the kitchen

■ NEW POTATO AND CHICKEN SALAD ■

Serves 4-6

- 30 ml (2 tablespoons) raspberry or red wine vinegar
- 75 ml (5 tablespoons) ale
- 45 ml (3 teaspoons) clear honey
- 23 ml (approx 1 ½ tablespoons) olive oil
- Salt and pepper
- 3 boneless chicken breasts, skinned and cut into strips
- 500 g (approx 1 lb 1oz) new potatoes, scrubbed and halved
- 200 g (7 oz) cherry tomatoes, halved
- ½ cucumber, diced
- 50 g (2 oz) bag rocket leaves
- Fresh raspberries to garnish

1 Combine 1 tablespoon vinegar, 2 tablespoons ale, 1 teaspoon honey, ½ tablespoon oil and the salt and pepper in a bowl and stir in the chicken.

2 Place the new potatoes in a pan of lightly salted boiling water. Cover and simmer for 15 minutes or until tender, then drain and allow to cool slightly. Mix with the tomatoes, cucumber and rocket.

3 Meanwhile heat a little oil in a large frying pan, remove the chicken from the marinade and stir-fry for 8-10 minutes or until cooked through and browned. Stir into the salad.

4 In the frying pan, heat the remaining vinegar, ale, honey, oil, salt and pepper and bring to the boil and reduce by half. Pour over the salad and toss well. Serve warm, garnished with fresh raspberries.

Recipe courtesy www.thinkvegetables.co.uk

■ AROUND THE HOUSE ■

Most of us have a shredder these days, to dispose of important documents such as bank statements. If you get a build-up of paper fragments in the cutters, unplug the shredder and use tweezers to pluck the bits out.

▎TOP TIP

Spray ice cubes with soda water before storing in a bag, to stop them freezing together.

Mr A Mundy, Farnham, Surrey

Great gardening
Calla Lily

Water gardens are becoming increasingly popular with gardeners because they provide so many different planting opportunities. One plant that thrives in moist soils – and even in water around 15 cm in depth – is the calla lily and several new cultivars have been produced recently. Three of the newest are 'Galaxy', 'Anneke' and 'Black Magic', which have vibrant red, purple and yellow flowers respectively. Natives of North America and Europe, they thrive in sun or partial shade and will add an elegant feel to any waterside planting scheme.

■ You can order plants from Unwins by visiting www.unwins-seeds.com

Superfood!

EAT MORE... MELON
Packed with...

Vitamin C, calcium, beta-carotene, phosphorus, magnesium and potassium.

Good for...

Re-hydrating and cleansing the body because of its high water content.

Get more by...

Serving up a seasonal fruity salad with your favourite fruits and a splash of freshly squeezed orange juice – or something stronger if you'd prefer! Alternatively, ball and serve in a meringue nest with a handful of raspberries and a sprig of mint.

My childhood home

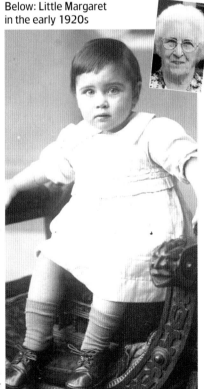

Below: Little Margaret in the early 1920s

I was born in 1919 in Holyhead, Anglesey, North Wales. Both my parents were Welsh speaking, so my first language was Welsh, and it wasn't until I went to school at five years old that I began learning English.

My first recollections are of living above the boot and shoe shop my father owned in Holyhead's main street.

There was a fitting room at the back of the shop and across one wall hung large pieces of leather which my father sold to those customers living in outlying villages who used to repair their own boots and shoes.

When I was about two, I was operated on for the removal of my adenoids and tonsils in the room above the shop.

Apparently the furniture was covered in sheets to make it as antiseptic as possible.

The shop next to ours was a milliner's and I remember the lovely hats displayed in the window. Opposite the shop was a large Saturday market; there were fruit and veg, knitting wool, clothes, farmers' and butchers' stalls. And the stall which sold homemade rock in all the colours of the rainbow – but it was the brown rock which tasted out of this world.

When darkness fell, the place would light up with flaming torches, and the noise and the smells would go on well past my bedtime.

Margaret Dormer, Richmond, Surrey

WINCHESTER: ANCIENT AND MODERN

Hat fair and history

Winchester is a treasure trove for lovers of antiquity. Its chief jewel is undoubtedly the 900-year-old cathedral but equally fascinating to historians are the legendary Arthurian Round Table, housed in the Great Hall of what remains of the castle, and the Hospital of St Cross medieval almshouse. At the bottom of the High Street flows the River Itchen where stands an ancient watermill that was rebuilt in 1744 and is now owned by the National Trust.

The story of Winchester, which started life as an important town in Roman times and was later rebuilt by King Alfred the Great, is traced in the City Museum. Scattered around the area are several museums that focus on military history, ranging from the Museum of the King's Royal Hussars to the Royal Green Jackets Museum and the Gurkha Museum.

Throughout the city, a modern note is struck by sculptures. A lifesize bronze of a horse and rider by Elizabeth Frink overlooks the High Street while in the cathedral square can be seen Luminous Motion, a stainless steel tower studded with changing coloured lights that creates a striking contrast with the ancient façade behind it.

Winchester's farmers' market, held on the first and last Sunday of every month, is said to be the largest in the country and has won the approval of chef Rick Stein for the variety and quality of the food on offer – including locally grown watercress.

An annual event in June and July is the Winchester Hat Fair, a festival of street theatre that takes its name from the money that onlookers throw into the hats of the performers.

Games on the green

Our village
Dorothy Hambelton of Lytham St Anne's recalls her brother coming a cropper on the village green

Directly opposite the side of our house in Royston, Yorkshire, was the village green. It was not the flat quadrangle one might expect of a village green but a long, downward sloping piece of land. There were bushes on one side where we played a game called barricades in which we kept out our raiding friends with cardboard boxes with spy holes cut into them.

One day as we were playing on the green my brother disappeared through the turf into a hole caused by mining subsidence. Fortunately, it was not very deep but it took a number of lorry loads of rubble and ashes to fill it before we were allowed to play on the green again.

There was a stream at the lower end of our road which Mother complained was the bane of her life. It drew local children like bees to a honey pot for we loved daring each other to jump over it and invariably one of us would land ankle-deep in mud.

Our annual day trip organised by the British Legion was one of the highlights of the summer. Several coaches full of excited children and parents travelled to Blackpool, Scarborough, Bridlington or Cleethorpes. My father would settle my mother on the beach and fasten a large Union Jack to her deckchair so we children knew where to return, should we wander off. The big moment of those outings was when each child was given a bag of rock and half-a-crown.

Local flower and vegetable shows were part of my childhood, too, as Dad was a keen amateur gardener. When he was presented with a medal by the Royal Horticultural Society, the local paper ran the headline, 'Great Britain's Best Garden, Royston Man Wins Premier Honour'.

Booming Eighties

PIC: REX FEATURES

1 Which New Romantic pop group had a hit with the song To Cut A Long Story Short?
A ABC
B Duran Duran
C Spandau Ballet
D Japan

2 What is the nationality of Erno Rubik, inventor of the Rubik's Cube?
A Hungarian
B Romanian
C French
D Greek

3 In the following list, which film was not directed by John Hughes?
A Pretty In Pink
B Uncle Buck
C The Breakfast Club
D Planes, Trains and Automobiles

4 In which year was the Australian soap opera Neighbours first shown in the UK?
A 1981
B 1986
C 1985
D 1988

5 Who won the 1980 British Formula One Grand Prix?
A Nelson Piquet
B Rene Arnoux
C Didier Pironi
D Alan Jones

6 What was the name of the first space shuttle to be launched?
A Challenger
B Enterprise
C Columbia
D Discovery

7 The first commercially available mobile phone appeared in 1983. Which company made it?
A Motorola
B Nokia
C Sony
D Siemens

8 What was the name of the final album by Sting's (above) former group, The Police?
A Every Breath You Take
B Sychronicity
C Ghost In The Machine
D Regatta De Blanc

9 What do the 'J' and 'R' stand for in the name JR Ewing?
A Joe Richard
B James Robert
C John Ross
D Joseph Ronald

10 Which of these popular comedies featured Back To The Future star Christopher Lloyd?
A Cheers
B Taxi
C Soap
D The Golden Girls

Answers: 1C, 2A, 3A, 4B, 5D, 6C, 7A, 8B, 9C, 10B

STRAWBERRY JAM

The summer show brings out the competitive spirit in a village's jam-makers

This year, Linda told herself, she would win first prize for strawberry jam. Not second, or third, or highly commended, but first.

Not that she was competitive. Oh no. She just wanted to beat Betsy Glen, who took first prize, year after year. Betsy was a paragon of a woman; she worked hard for local charities, her home was always sparkling clean, her children well behaved. And she made the best stawberry jam in the village.

Linda was tired of always being the runner-up. Okay, so it was only the local summer show, and what was a jar of jam? Pretty unimportant in the great scheme of things. Still, it would be nice to see that first prize rosette. So Linda took special care with her jam making.

Her first batch wasn't up to scratch but she had high hopes for her second attempt. The strawberries were just right. "No, you can't come into the kitchen, I'm busy," she snapped at her younger son, Ben, when he wanted to use the table for making a model plane.

"Oh, please, Mum."

"I said no. Do it somewhere else."

Ben, hurt, took himself off. Usually Mum liked helping to make models, and never minded a bit of a mess on the kitchen table.

Linda scanned the recipe which was taken from an old book on home craft. When the jam was nearly done, she spooned a little on to a chilled saucer. She pushed gently with her finger as it cooled and watched the surface crinkle. Just right.

She poured the jam into three jars, put a disc of waxed paper on top, then covered them. After storing them in the larder, she decided to print the labels on the computer to give a professional touch.

"Mum, I'm bored."

"Already? You've only been on holiday a week."

"Could I have the kitchen table, and an old cornflakes packet to make another model?"

Linda was tired of always being the runner-up

"All right."

Linda went into the study and turned on the computer. It was then she heard the crash.

"I was only reaching for the cornflakes packet!" Ben looked guilty.

"What have you done?"

Linda's heart sank as she saw the debris – the broken glass, the sticky mess on the floor, the remains of what had been three prize-winning jars of strawberry jam. She trod carefully through the glass.

"Out of the way, please!" Ben, fearing an explosion, disappeared. Linda screamed silently, then began to mop up the sorry remains.

"It doesn't matter," she said when she'd recovered her temper, "It's only jam."

"You make very good jam," said Pete, when he came home that evening.

"But this was special. It was for the show. I'll just have to put in a pot from the first batch I made even though it wasn't nearly so good."

"Well, the first batch won't be wasted. We'll eat anything!"

She threw the tea towel at him and said it was his turn to wash up. The children grinned – Mum was back to her own self again.

On the evening before the show, Linda placed her jar in the section marked Jams and Jellies. Well, it looked good, anyway – she was pleased with the artistic label. Then Betsy appeared, carrying a basket from which she produced several pots of jelly and one of strawberry jam.

"Hello," she greeted Linda, "Who's going to win this year?"

"I'm sure you will," Linda replied through gritted teeth.

"Oh no, my dear, you make lovely jam! Well, we'll see what the judges think, won't we?"

FOREVER

BY ANNE FORSYTH

TimSharville.com

Linda made her escape. Next day, she arrived at the hall soon after the show opened, and wandered round, greeting friends and admiring the flowers and vegetables. At last she couldn't wait any longer and made her way to Jams and Jellies.

Yes, there were the entries in the strawberry jam class. She felt a pang of disappointment when she saw the ticket beside her jar. Only a second. Oh, well, she hadn't really expected a first.

"Goodness me!" Betsy's voice came from behind her. "A mere third."

Together they gazed disbelievingly at Betsy's jar.

"I wonder who won?" Betsy peered closer at the label. "It's a

Oh, well, she hadn't really expected a first

man! Would you believe it?"

Another friend leaned over to look. "It's old Mr Andrews. You know, lives on his own. He's a very good cook."

Betsy and Linda looked at each other. "Well done, my dear," Betsy said, "A second. And your label looks most professional."

Linda began to laugh. "You know, I didn't think mine was worth a prize at all." And she told Betsy what had happened.

"That's boys for you!" Betsy laughed and launched into a story of how her eldest had once broken

a precious china ornament on a visit to an elderly aunt.

"But I thought your family were always perfectly behaved."

"Don't you believe it," Betsy smiled broadly, and Linda warmed to her.

"Then there's hope for my lot," she grinned.

"Come on," said Betsy, "let's see what else our Mr Andrews has won. We're up against stiff competition here."

"There he is," Linda spotted an elderly man in the centre of a little group admiring a Victoria sponge. "Let's go and congratulate him."

"We can always ask him for his strawberry jam recipe," Betsy winked. "He might pass on the secret!"

Friday

I
Edinburgh Military Tattoo begins

Saturday

2
National Eisteddfod of Wales begins

Sunday

3

Monday

4
Summer Bank Holiday (Scotland)

Tuesday

5

Wednesday

6

Thursday

7

Friday

8

Saturday

9

Sunday

IO

Monday

II

Tuesday

I2
Yours magazine on sale

Wednesday

I3

Thursday

I4

Friday

I5

Saturday

I6

Sunday

I7

Monday

I8

Tuesday

I9

Wednesday

20

Thursday

2I

Friday

22

Saturday # 23	Thursday # 28
Sunday # 24	Friday # 29
Monday # 25 Summer Bank Holiday (Except Scotland)	Saturday # 30
Tuesday # 26 Yours magazine on sale	Sunday # 31
Wednesday # 27	

PIC: REX FEATURES

Born this month

American film star Robert Redford was born on August 18, 1936, in California. He shot to fame in his role as the Sundance Kid in the 1969 film Butch Cassidy and the Sundance Kid.

Married this month

Beautiful Vivien Leigh (pictured), best known for her role as Scarlett O'Hara in Gone With The Wind (1939) married actor Laurence Olivier on August 31,1940. They fell in love while making the film Fire Over England (1937).

Died this month

The death of Diana, Princess of Wales, in a car accident in a Paris road tunnel, along with Dodi Al-Fayed and driver Henri Paul, on August 31, 1997 shocked the world. Diana's final resting place is in the grounds of Althorp Park, her family home.

My childhood home

Oaklands was a large three-storey semi-detached house in Berkhamstead and it had a disused stable block in the garden. My friends and I played for hours in the hayloft. This meant we had to climb up the wall ladder and we were very scared of stepping on to the first rung when we were climbing down. My wonderful mother would bring us snacks in plastic bowls, balanced on an upturned broom.

We had a large kitchen and a small scullery with a stone container for washing clothes and a large mangle. I can remember 'Old John' the weekly gardener sitting on a wooden chair in the scullery drinking his mug of tea. I was scared of him because he had a hairy face.

My most vivid memories of my childhood days at Oakland were the wonderful tennis parties my parents gave, together with the people from the adjoining house, which also had a grass court. There would be such laughter and enjoyment. At the tea break my mother would provide a splendid tea with home-made cakes. One of my proudest moments was when I was considered old enough to take the silver

Lucy, aged three years, in 1941

water jug to the kitchen to refill it.

The house is now demolished to make way for new housing, but no demolition can take away my childhood memories.

**Lucy Lester,
Leighton Buzzard**

Great gardening

Dahlias

When it comes to late summer colour, few plants beat dahlias for vibrancy. Originating in central and southern America, the humble dahlia has come a long way since it was first grown, thanks to a number of extensive breeding programmes – there are now thousands of cultivars to choose from, hundreds of different flower colours and shapes. One of the newer cultivars is 'Rita Shrimpton', the first double collerette cultivar ever released.

■ Plants are available as rooted cuttings during the spring and can be ordered, tel: 01736 335 851 or www.wgltd.co.uk

TOP TIP

When going on holiday, share your family's clothes between the suitcases. If one case is lost, at least everyone will have something to wear.

Tessa Hunt, Exeter

In the kitchen

MINTY BROAD BEAN DIP

Serves 4-6
- 200 g (7 oz) podded broad beans
- 200 g (7 oz) Greek yoghurt
- Small handful of mint leaves
- 20 g (approx 1 oz) Pecorino cheese, grated (or Parmesan)
- ½ clove garlic, crushed (optional)
- Salt and pepper
- A selection of vegetable crudités – carrots, cucumber, celery, peppers, radishes, lettuce – to serve

1 Cook the broad beans in a pan of boiling water for about 4-5 minutes. Drain and rinse under cold water. Shell the beans and discard the skins, if necessary. Very small young beans will be fine as they are.
2 Put the beans, yoghurt, mint, cheese and garlic (if using) into a food processor. Whizz until you have a thick green purée. Season to taste.
3 Serve the dip with a selection of colourful vegetable crudités.

Recipe courtesy The English Pea & Bean Season

We remember when...

The Queen Mother celebrated her 100th birthday on August 4, 2000, to celebrations around the country. She was the first member of the Royal Family to reach her centenary and received a congratulatory handwritten telegram from Buckingham Palace from the Queen!

A Grand Day Out

Summer Sundays in the late 1940s, early 50s were my favourite, family fun days. Preparation began on Saturday afternoon when Dad packed our tent in the sidecar – plus tent pegs, guy ropes, mallet, bicycle pump and puncture repair kit. Mum baked apple pies, fluffy Victoria sponges and sultana scones.

Early on Sunday morning, Tommy, my younger brother, would climb into the sidecar jammed between the tent paraphernalia and picnic, then Dad climbed on the bicycle and they'd be away to Crosby beach, near Liverpool.

Mum and I followed by train. I can still feel the atmosphere, the smell of candy floss, the shops thronged with visitors, the roadside edged with buckets filled with coloured plastic windmills.

By the time we arrived at the beach, Dad had the tent up, yellow silk flag flying high – it was the only way to find your tent, as there were so many on the beach.

These were long, hot, fun days – kite flying, paddling, queuing for pots of tea at the beach café.

At the end of the day, Mum would run a warm bath for us, and rub our sun-reddened skin in calomine lotion before she tucked us into bed.

Pauline O'Keeffe, Parbold, Lancs

Superfood!

EAT MORE... CUCUMBER

Packed with...

Beta-carotene and potassium.

Good for...

Aiding digestion, regulating blood pressure and helping prevent kidney and bladder stones. Also thought to have a laxative effect.

Get more by...

Cutting into batons to eat with salsa or dipping in a cheese fondue. Alternatively, make a cucumber dip by whipping together some thick cream, 4 squeezes of lemon juice, finely chopped cucumber and ¼ of an onion.

In the kitchen

SWEET FLAN

Serves 6-8

- 200 g (7 oz) caster sugar
- Zest and juice of 1 lemon
- 600 ml (approx 1 pint) milk
- Zest of 1 orange
- 3 large eggs
- 3 large egg yolks
- Orange segments to decorate

1 Preheat the oven to 170°C, 325°F or Gas Mark 3. Place 175 g (6 oz) of the caster sugar in a pan and gently heat, stirring until the sugar dissolves.

2 Add the lemon juice and stir until the bubbling stops.

3 Pour into a 900 ml (approx 1½ pt) round heatproof dish, swirl to spread the caramel over the base and sides. Set aside.

4 Add the milk to the caramel pan, with the lemon and orange zest. Slowly bring to the boil. Leave to cool, then strain and discard zest. Beat the eggs, egg yolks and remaining sugar together, then beat in the milk.

5 Pour the egg mixture over the caramel lined dish. Place the dish in a roasting tin, then pour boiling water from the kettle to come halfway up the outside of the dish. Bake for 35-40 mins or until just set but still a little wobbly in the centre. Cool. Chill for at least 4 hours.

6 Meanwhile, segment the orange and reserve. To serve, invert the pudding onto a serving plate, cut into wedges and decorate with the orange segments.

Recipe courtesy Lion Quality Eggs

Superfood!

EAT MORE... PINEAPPLE

Packed with...

Manganese, vitamins B1, B6 and C, thiamin, calcium, copper, bromelain, phosphorus, fibre, potassium and beta-carotene.

Good for...

A healthy brain and nervous system and protecting against macular degeneration. The potent digestive enzyme bromelain is thought to reduce bacteria and parasites too.

Get more by...

Dicing and mixing with finely chopped chilli peppers for a tangy salsa or cutting into rings, sprinkling with ground cinnamon or ginger and charring on a griddle pan. Alternatively, blend and freeze – it's a treat rivalling ice-cream!

We remember when...

Six years of war finally ended as Japan surrendered to the Allies on August 15, 1945. Germany had surrendered nearly four months before but fighting between the Allies and Japan continued until two atomic bombs were dropped by America on Hiroshima and Nagasaki. August 15 was named Victory in Japan day.

AROUND THE HOUSE

It's easy to succumb to dehydration during the summer. When you're out, always keep a small bottle of water handy. And when the bottle's finished, use it to water plants that are too fiddly for the watering can.

A Grand Day Out

A s a child my holiday each year was the annual Sunday School outing, the destination alternating each year between Barry Island and Porthcawl.

We so looked forward to it and there was great excitement as to who would be the first to see the sea.

Then straight on to the beach, making sandcastles, paddling and eating our picnic. I always had to take some seaweed home for Dad because he said he could tell what the weather was like when he hung it in the porch. Before we set off for home, we were treated to fish and chips – in the paper, of course! Happy memories.

**Joan Fishbourne,
Hereford**

Twelve-year-old Joan in 1949 (centre, behind littlest boy) with family and friends at the fairground

My childhood home

Rosemary's childhood home

M y Mother loved our bungalow in Bradford. It represented the most important things in her life – her family, home-making and good food. She was proud of the modernisation she and Dad had done to make the bungalow special and she would be puzzled to know that none of these things are best remembered by me.

It was the wooden lean-to shed that holds a piece of my heart, even now. On the day Dad cleared his tools from the lean-to to the garage, the shed became mine – all four feet square of it.

I dusted the shelf and swept the floor. I found a cardboard box and filled it with newspapers for the cat to sleep in. Decorations were a jam jar of flowers and the pictures I'd drawn. I was about seven years old.

Cat and I spent many happy hours in the shed, and I would read aloud to him. Gradually the shed fell apart, I married and moved away. My parents died and the bungalow was sold.

When I retired I bought myself

Mi'Ut, 2000

a hut and put it up in the garden. Christened 'Mi Ut'. There's room for an armchair, used by the present Cat, and I sit at a small table to write or paint. Flowers are now in a fancy jug and there are net curtains at the windows but the purpose is still the same. My hideaway.

**Rosemary Nattriss, Tadcaster,
N Yorks**

Great gardening

Pelargoniums

G ardeners who love pelargoniums know that few growers are as well-respected as the Sulmans, Brian and Pearl, who've specialised in breeding these plants for many years. One of their newest introductions is the Regal pelargonium 'Royal Prince' with upper petals of raspberry red, lower petals of light pink and a white centre. Raised by Mrs Nicola Stemp, the Sulmans have tested it extensively and are now releasing it to the market. Summer container plants don't get much better than this!

■ You can order plants – the minimum order is ten plants, but not all of one variety – by calling 01638 712 297 or visiting www.sulmanspelargoniums.co.uk

A Grand Day Out

My friend and I decided we would go out on a day trip to one of my favourite places – Haworth in Yorkshire, home of the Brontë sisters. It was a beautiful sunny day and the scenery was stunning (I may be prejudiced here as, although I live in Lincolnshire, I'm from Yorkshire).

We looked around the little shops, went down the steep hill to the pretty park to eat our picnic and relaxed in the hot sunshine.

We could have stayed longer but we heard the sound of morris men at the top of the hill so, being fans of morris dancing, went to see them perform.

There were many people milling around watching them, and the morris men and ladies were a mass of colours – so lovely in the sunshine.

One of them kindly took my photograph, and he lent me his hat to wear. I have very special memories of a lovely day every time I look at the photo.

Barbara Finch, Chapel St Leonards, Lincs

Barbara, morris dancing's newest recruit

TOP TIP

Having had my ears pierced in 2006 (at the age of 65!) I buy new earrings at every opportunity! To save time having to search for a matching pair in my earring box, I've put a piece of foam in the bottom and stick them in, in pairs. Much easier to find.

Brenda Edson, Basildon, Essex

In the kitchen

■ CAJUN SPICED SWEET POTATO WEDGES ■
Serves 6

- ■ 4 large sweet potatoes, scrubbed
- ■ 45 ml (3 tablespoons) olive oil
- ■ 45 ml (3 tablespoons) Cajun seasoning
- ■ 200 ml (approx 7 fl oz) tzatziki to serve

1 Preheat oven to 220°C, 425°F or Gas Mark 7. Slice each sweet potato in half lengthways, then each half into 3 to make fat wedges

2 Mix the oil and Cajun seasoning in a small bowl. Brush the mixture over the flesh of the sweet potatoes.

3 Transfer the sweet potatoes to a non-stick roasting tin and bake for 20-25 minutes.

4 Serve with tzatziki.

Recipe courtesy www.thinkvegetables.co.uk

We remember when...

Two penguins from Chessington Zoo were taken to a local ice rink to cool off this week in 1967, as Britain sweltered in a heatwave. Rockhopper penguins feel the heat more than other species and zoo keepers were worried they were suffering in the high temperatures. At Streatham ice rink in London the two skated around the rink with other skaters – and seemed to be having a great time!

Great gardening

Salvia

One plant that appears regularly at all the trendiest flower shows is the salvia – whether grown for its leaves or flowers. A newer cultivar, 'Dot's Delight,' makes a great plant, vigorously producing blue and white flowers all summer. It's a real breakthrough, because it's thought to be the first bi-coloured cultivar created using salvia patens as a parent.

■ You can order it from the Hardy's Cottage Garden Plants, tel: 01256 896 533 or www.hardys-plants.co.uk

▨ AROUND THE HOUSE ▨

If the sun has dried your skin out, dab pure almond oil on your face once or twice a week. It will feel wonderful as it replenishes your skin's natural oils.

Superfood!

▨ EAT MORE... PEAS
Packed with...

B vitamins, iron, zinc, potassium, folic acid, calcium and magnesium.

Good for...

Aiding liver function and boosting energy.

Get more by...

Adding to pasta, rice dishes and omelettes. Also great with cheese, especially in sandwiches – cook and mash peas, mix with mayonnaise and grated cheese, spread on buttered bread and enjoy!

My childhood home

Molly's childhood home in Stanford-le-Hope

From 1935, this was my childhood home in Stanford-le-Hope, Essex. The shop had been added in 1920 but the house was much older and featured on postcards of the village.

The sitting room had wood panelling, most rooms had oak beams and the staircase to the bedroom was in the wall behind the dresser in the scullery.

The outside walls were very thick and I could sit on the windowsills and draw the curtains behind me. It was a lovely creaky old house lit by gas and at Christmas it was magic.

It has been demolished now and the house and

garden is a row of houses, but when I go past I imagine it's still there, and there's a child playing with the dogs in the garden.

Molly Barnett, Grays, Essex

My childhood home

I was born and grew up in a detached house in Old Earley, near Reading, from the mid 1940s, together with my elder sister, Sally. The house was designed and built by my Mother's brother, there being only one other identical – being his own – in Maidenhead.

My Father was a policeman in Reading Borough Police, based in Valpy Street. We had a huge back garden which was divided up into a lawned area, flower garden, greenhouse, fruit trees and vegetable garden, Dad's onion patch – and his pride and joy – being at the end.

Our house had a big porch with red tiles and big terracotta gryphon sitting in front of it, which was always admired by Vicar Robinson. One day, when he came to visit, he missed the step leading into the front room and went headlong, only stopping at the far wall!

The Vicar had always admired the gryphon (which we called 'the devil') and one day Mum decided it should go, so he went away, pleased as punch, with it in his car. Only she could have got him to go off with the devil… I often wonder if it's still in the vicarage garden.

Diane Vaughan, Didcot, Oxon

Diane (far right) next to big sister Sally in their back garden

Great gardening

Verbena

Verbena 'Seabrook's Lavender' was a chance seedling that Peter Seabrook found in his Essex garden. It has proved hardy after over-wintering for more than seven years and has lavender-coloured blooms with a pretty, deeper eye. A short-lived perennial, it produces a mound of mid-green leaves around 38cm in height. Cut it hard back after flowering and it will quickly re-grow. It flowers freely between May and December, making it excellent in containers.

■ To order, tel: 01256 896 533 or www.hardys-plants.co.uk

Superfood!

EAT MORE… PEARS

Packed with…

Vitamins C and K, fibre, calcium, magnesium, copper, folic acid, iodine, beta-carotene, fibre and potassium.

Good for…

Keeping the bowels regular and maintaining a normal thyroid function. This energy-boosting snack can also help regulate blood pressure and aid the removal of toxins from the body.

Get more by…

Coring and poaching in apple juice or wine, chopping into your breakfast porridge with a spoon of honey or mixing with watercress and walnuts for a crunchy sweet salad.

■ AROUND THE HOUSE ■

Keep some of the water next time you defrost your freezer, for use in your steam iron.

In the kitchen

STRAWBERRY OAT CRUMBLE

Serves 6

- 700 g (1¹/₂ lb) strawberries
- 140 g (approx 5 oz) unrefined demerara sugar
- 110 g (4 oz) plain wholemeal flour
- 85 g (approx 3 oz) butter
- 1 teaspoon freshly ground black pepper
- 100 g (3¹/₂ oz) macadamia nuts
- 50 g (2 oz) rolled porridge oats

1 Preheat the oven to 200°C, 400°F or Gas Mark 6. Place the strawberries in a 20 cm (8 in) x 25 cm (10 in) ovenproof dish and sprinkle over 30 g (approx 1 oz) of the demerara sugar.
2 In a food processor whiz together the flour, remaining sugar and butter until combined. Add the pepper, nuts and oats and pulse until the nuts are roughly chopped.
3 Tip the crumble mix over the strawberries, spread out evenly and press down. Use a fork to loosen the top a little and bake in the oven for 35 minutes until golden. Serve with clotted cream or custard.

Recipe courtesy Billington's and Allinson

We remember when...

We could finally shop on Sundays, as Sunday trading laws were lifted this week in 1994 and thousands of shops opened for the first time on Sunday. Small shops were allowed to open all day, while larger stores were restricted to six hours of opening time. Some shops and church groups were opposed to the change, but for many who worked difficult hours, it made things easier.

A Grand Day Out

I know this isn't really a day out, but it is a lasting holiday memory I wanted to share. As a little girl in the 1950s I was very lucky to go on a cruise each year with my Auntie Birdie. She was in her sixties, with white hair and seemed very old to a six-year-old but she was so kind. She was unmarried and we enjoyed each other's company and I was excited to go away without my parents.

We would get a bus to the docks and haul our suitcases along the jetty. I was always terrified I would slip between the planks and fall into the sea.

Once on board we would go and get a cup of tea for Auntie Birdie and a cream soda with a block of ice cream in it for me. Our cruise seemed to last

forever but eventually we reached our destination… Margate. Our trip on board the Royal Daffodil from Gravesend was over.

We spent several idyllic days at the Hollywood Hotel in Westbrooke overlooking the sea, and which had its own private garden with steps leading down to the sea. What luxury!

I remember having Tutti-Frutti ice cream and trips to Dreamland where I used to have candy floss which used to get stuck in my long, curly hair.

The trip from Gravesend to Margate would now take all of half an hour by car but what an adventure it was then for a small girl.

**Jean Spain,
Sittingbourne, Kent**

Jean and Auntie Birdie on Westbrooke beach in 1950

BRISTOL: ANCIENT AND MODERN

Blue glass and balloons

Big merchant ships used to sail right into the heart of Bristol until the 1870s when changes in the river levels meant the docks had to be relocated to the mouth of the Avon. Now the harbourside area is a vibrant 21st century mix of shops, cafés and galleries by day with clubs and restaurants coming to life after dark.

Foodies adore Bordeaux Quay which combines a restaurant, brasseries, bar, deli, bakery and cooking school under one roof. On the first Sunday of every month, they can be found buying the best of local foods from the stalls at St Nicholas Market.

The city has some fascinating museums including the British Empire and Commonwealth Museum which is housed in Temple Meads old station, designed by Isambard Kingdom Brunel. The Victorian engineer was also behind the world's first propellor-driven iron ship, the SS Great Britain. Salvaged in 1970, the liner was towed back to the Bristol dockyard where she was originally built and is now open to the public.

Glass has long been associated with this city

and Bristol Blue Glass is still made at the factory in Brislington where you can see glass being blown.

Theatre lovers should be sure to book ahead to see a production at Bristol Old Vic which is situated in a complex that includes the 1766 Theatre Royal in cobbled King Street. Drama of a different kind can be seen every August when over 100 hot air balloons float over the city for its annual International Balloon Festival. They provide an unforgettable spectacle as they glide above the Avon Gorge and the Clifton Suspension Bridge, another of Brunel's legacies to the largest city in the south-west.

Bilberry pie for supper

Happy times in the Pennine village of Norland are recalled by Pat Paine of Chippenham, Wiltshire

Our village

Blackberry time coincided with the school summer holidays so on a fine day Mother and I would pack some sandwiches, take a shopping basket, and walk to a lane that was lined with blackberry bushes. We spent a few hours filling our baskets before eating our sandwiches and catching the lunchtime bus home. Mother would then be busy cleaning and weighing the many pounds of blackberries before making them into jam, or bottling them, for the store cupboard.

Another summer pastime was to take an empty jam jar to fill

with bilberries from the bushes growing on the moor, not too far from the roadway. After an hour or two of picking I would return home, sometimes with the jar still only partly full of these tiny juicy fruits. Mother always made a delicious pie that stained your mouth a deep purple colour.

Summer and winter, the postman never missed a day's delivery. Starting the day in Sowerby Post Office, he would climb the steep hillside on foot, delivering mail as he went. If anyone was sick, he'd gladly take their prescription to the chemist and deliver the medicine on his

rounds the following day. He was sadly missed when he retired and his round was taken over by a postman in a van.

Occasionally on Saturday evenings a dance would be held in the village school. The partition between the two classrooms was pulled back and, although many of the men were away in the forces, most of the village folk attended to enjoy waltzes, quicksteps and The Lancers. At the end of the evening, my mother and I walked over a mile home with only the stars to light our way as no street lighting was allowed in wartime.

The Rook

John Phillpott remembers a special spring in 1958

"He won't live, boy. Better put him back in the spinney. His mother will look after him." Uncle George strides ahead, that distinctive gait taking on the kind of urgency that shouts annoyance with every step.

If I've irritated him, I'm not aware of it. But when you're aged nine and bursting with questions for a weary 55-year-old, the last thing on your mind is whether or not you've become a nuisance.

Late April, 1958. It's a balmy evening, yet winter's breath is still all around, reluctant to hand over the reins to spring.

Uncle George gives me the sideways glance that means his mood might be mellowing. I look down at the jet-black bundle with coal eyes. Kaa-aak! says the bundle. And then a peck to my hand by way of protest. Meet the rook. No. Meet my rook.

Uncle George, say I, there's no point in putting him back into the spinney. How will he fly back to his nest? And if I leave him on the spinney floor, won't a fox, stoat or badger eat him?

I study Uncle George's sun-burned face.

He's the farm labourer who lives in the cottage over the road and not really my uncle.

Anyway, I think he's softened. He looks at the rook and smiles. Suddenly, he plunges his alder stick into the dried crust of a cow pat, and deftly takes off the top to reveal yellowing grass and a mass of squirming leatherjackets. He scoops up a handful of these grey-brown grubs and unceremoniously rams a few into the rook's gaping beak.

Uncle George eyes the bird: "If it's not dead by morning it should live. Feed it on chopped worms, bread, milk, beetles, spiders…

He looks at the rook and smiles

anything you can find." That night, my new friend – Rookie – is found new lodgings in the old pig sty. The next morning, I'm up early before school and digging for worms. Rookie is ravenous. At break time, I run home to attend to him. As soon as the school bell rings for home time, I'm through the gate to search for more worms.

The next day's the same, and the next. Days turn into weeks, weeks into months.

But things are changing. Rookie's growing up, his pin quills splitting to reveal the feathers of an adult bird. And one day he'll have to be given his freedom.

But not just yet. And so I walk the rolling fields around my north Warwickshire village home with my good friend the rook. I become the bird-boy of Churchover.

The fateful day arrives. One sultry evening in late August my mother and I start the sad journey to the spinney where Rookie had been born those few months before.

Now is the time. Rookie flutters to the top of the tallest willow by the pond. We turn and walk back to the village, my mother staring straight ahead, while my eyes stream with tears. And then I remember Uncle George's words that Sunday evening in faraway April.

He won't live, boy. But he did, Uncle George, he did.

PIC: REX FEATURES

Monday

1

Tuesday

2

Wednesday

3

Thursday

4

Friday

5

Saturday

6

Sunday

7

Monday

8

Tuesday

9

Yours magazine on sale

Wednesday

10

Thursday

11

Friday

12

Saturday

13

Sunday

14

Monday

15

Battle of Britain Day

Tuesday

16

Wednesday

17

Thursday

18

Friday

19

Saturday

20

Sunday

21

Monday

22

Tuesday **23**	Saturday **27**
Wednesday **24**	Sunday **28**
Thursday **25**	Monday **29**
Friday **26**	Tuesday **30**

Yours magazine on sale

PIC: REX FEATURES

Born this month

Sixties supermodel, Twiggy, was born on September 19, 1949. She was born Leslie Hornby and was nicknamed Twiggy because of her slender figure.

Married this month

Italian actress Sophia Loren (pictured) married film producer Carlo Ponti on September 17, 1957. Carlo had arranged a Mexican divorce from his Italian first wife, as divorce was illegal in Italy. But when he was told he'd be charged with bigamy if he returned to Italy, his marriage to Sophia was annulled. They remarried in April 1966.

Died this month

Mother Teresa died on September 5, 1997, nine days after her 87th birthday. Throughout her life she'd selflessly looked after those in need, helping the sick and dying.

A Grand Day Out

It was a lovely sunny morning in September 1939 and Mam and Dad were taking me to Walney Island, which was quite a long walk from where we lived in Barrow. But I didn't care. I was nearly eight and had just made my first Holy Communion, and felt so happy and grown up.

"It's so hot, can I wear my bathing costume?"

"We'll see," said Mam, who was making Spam sandwiches. I was so excited and started running around the living room, and singing at the top of my voice.

"Be quiet," said Dad. He'd just put the wireless on, and a man was talking. "Mr Chamberlain has said there's a war started."

"There's a war every year," I said cheekily.

"No, you're thinking of Armistice Day. That's remembering people in the 1914-1918 war. Now we're going to have another war and fight against Hitler." I'd heard of him and thought he had funny hair and moustache.

"Come on," said Mam and after a long, tiring walk we arrived at the lovely sandy beach. I paddled in the cool water and made sandcastles. But then the tide came in and they disappeared – now that did upset me.

Marie Goodwin, Morecambe, Lancs

Marie in her confirmation dress, 1939

Great gardening

Streptocarpus

Our gardens may be packed with plants from different parts of the world, but some need a warmer climate if they're to survive. One plant which requires winter heat is the streptocarpus, as it comes from Africa. However, it's worth the expense because it flowers abundantly for weeks. No one has done more to boost its popularity than Dibleys Nurseries, with a recent release – 'Chloe' – which has pale pink petals with rich red-purple veins across the lower lobes.
■ To order, visit www.dibleys.com

Superfood!

EAT MORE... SPINACH

Packed with...

Vitamins A, C, E, B2, B1, B6 and K, manganese, folate, iron, calcium, phosphorus, zinc, selenium, fibre and folic acid.

Good for...

Helping brain function by aiding mental performance, memory and stabilising mood. May also help protect against age-related illnesses, such as macular degeneration, arthritis and osteoporosis.

Get more by...

Adding to lasagne, serving as a side salad with a twist of lemon, or steaming with crushed garlic and olive oil and topping with grated parmesan.

In the kitchen

PORK FILLET WITH APPLE SALSA

- 450 g (1 lb) pork fillet, trimmed
- 100 ml (3 fl oz) cider
- 1 tablespoon Fruisana fruit sugar
- 5 ml (1 teaspoon) English mustard
- 2 cloves garlic, peeled and crushed
- 2 teaspoons fresh thyme leaves
- 30 ml (2 tablespoons) olive oil
- Juice and zest of 1 lemon

Salsa
- Zest and juice of 1 lemon
- 60mls (4 tablespoons) cider
- 50g (2ozs) sultanas
- 1 teaspoon fresh thyme leaves
- 2 dessert apples
- Salt and freshly ground black pepper

1 Cut the fillets into 1 cm (⅓ in) rounds.

2 Mix together the cider, Fruisana, mustard, garlic, thyme, olive oil and lemon zest and juice and mix well. Pour over the pork. Cover and chill until needed.

3 For the salsa, place the lemon zest, 2 tablespoons lemon juice, cider, sultanas and thyme leaves in a small mixing bowl. Peel, core and finely dice the apples and add to the mixture, coat well. Season.

4 Season the meat, place in preheated frying pan and cook for 3 minutes each side.

5 Serve with the apple salsa, sautéed potatoes and seasonal vegetables.   Recipe courtesy Fruisana

AROUND THE HOUSE

Be crafty – an empty toothbrush case is ideal for storing crochet hooks, and keep a magnet handy for errant pins and sewing needles.

My childhood home

I came into the world in the early hours of February 24, 1949, in a tiny cottage in Great Offley, Hertfordshire and lived there until I was six. The cottage was number four in a row of five, opposite the Methodist Chapel.

You walked straight into the living room from the outside, and there was the black range. I can remember sitting in front of it at the table, eating a boiled egg, fresh from a neighbour's chickens – with soldiers. Often there would be a little dress for my dolly which my Mum had got for me, on the table.

My very small bedroom was over the kitchen – I can remember that we had a rat in the house which used to live in a cupboard under the stairs, and I could hear it gnawing at night. Mum tried everything to get rid of it, which we did eventually.

I had a very happy time living in the cottage, and loved going to tea with Aunt Patty who lived next door. She had the most beautiful paper-thin china cups and saucers (all odd sets) and I loved drinking tea and eating wafer thin slices of bread and butter with her homemade redcurrant jelly.

Although the cottage no longer exists, I have many happy memories of living there and, best of all, I still have my lovely Mum.

Mrs Judy Evans, Luton

We remember when...

Britain and France declared war on Germany on September 3, 1939, following the invasion of Poland two days previously. The war had far reaching consequences: Rationing, evacuation of children to the countryside and the need for women to work in the factories and on the land meant that life would never be the same again.

In the kitchen

RASPBERRY AND CINNAMON MUFFINS

Makes 12
- 275 g (10 oz) plain flour
- 20 ml (4 teaspoons) baking powder
- Pinch of salt
- 5 ml (1 teaspoon) ground cinnamon
- 100 g (approx 4 oz) butter, melted
- 2 large eggs, beaten
- 100 g (approx 4 oz) caster sugar
- 175 ml (6 fl oz) milk
- 225 g (8 oz) frozen raspberries, thawed

1 Preheat the oven to 190°C, 375°F or Gas Mark 5. Line a 12 hole muffin tray with paper cake cases.

2 Sift the flour, baking powder, salt and cinnamon into a large bowl and make a well in the centre.

3 Beat the butter, eggs, sugar and milk together. Pour the milk mix into the dry ingredients with the raspberries and lightly mix together – do not over mix.

3 Divide the mixture between the muffin cases and bake for 30-35 minutes or until golden and risen. Cool in the tin for 5 minutes, then serve either warm or cold.

Recipe courtesy Lion Quality Eggs

TOP TIP

Put some safety pins on your key ring for emergencies.   **Mrs C Corbett, Birmingham**

We remember when...

American Express opened their credit card service in Britain this week in 1963. There was an annual fee of £3 12s for the cards. But it was the introduction of Barclaycard in 1966 that made the idea of credit cards more popular. And according to some sources, there are now more credit cards in the UK than there are people!

AROUND THE HOUSE

If you've made jam, don't store it on the top shelf in the kitchen as the rising heat may make it ferment.

Superfood!

EAT MORE... ONIONS

Packed with...

Chromium, vitamins B6 and C, iodine, potassium, tryphophan, potassium, calcium, folate, magnesium, folic acid and antioxidants sulfur and quercetin.

Good for...

Helping to raise levels of 'good' HDL cholesterol and reducing inflammation inside the body, as onions have a naturally antiseptic effect. They also help neutralise toxic cells, which may cause diseases such as cancer.

Get more by...

Chopping into salads, sandwiches and rice dishes. Alternatively, mix with chopped tomatoes, avocado and jalapeno peppers to make a guacamole dip.

My childhood home

The house where I was born and lived in until I was 12 years old, was 60 Hall Street, Burslem, Stoke-on-Trent.

The hall had a tile floor, with brown leather wallpaper which came halfway up. The parlour was for special occasions and the sitting room had a large black lead fireplace, a table and chairs, a sideboard, a wind-up gramophone and wireless and two large fireside chairs.

The house was at the back of Wades pot bank, and there was also what we call in Stoke-on-Trent, a shoredruck, which was where they threw the pottery that was no good.

Gillian Wain, Stoke-on-Trent

Gillian on the step at No. 60

A Grand Day Out

I had many trips out with my grandparents, and fond memories of being taken to the zoo, Tower Bridge, the old Chiswick Empire and Shepherd's Bush Empire by aunts and uncles, and my parents. I realise how lucky I was that they engendered in me a love of travel, theatre and music…

We were off! Red sandals shining and a white bow in my hair, my nan and granddad were taking me on a summer coach trip to the seaside from their home in London.

We'd sit in the back with a packet of barley twists to stop my travel sickness. As soon as we were on board, out would come the sandwiches, apples and flasks of tea.

On this occasion it was Southend and, after a dash for the toilets, the next stop was the bucket and spade shop and after that, the beach – but only to find that the tide was out.

I emerged from under a towel in my bright pink swimsuit. Nan took off her shoes and stockings and tucked up her skirt into her knicker leg elastic and with granddad looking after the bags, she walked me out over muddy sand, worm casts squelching between our toes, to where there was some sea left to play in.

After the long walk back, Nan discovered that my dip in the sea had left me covered in a black tarry substance. I had to suffer the indignity of having my swimsuit removed while Nan tried to scrub it off my bottom before being dressed again and given some sandwiches!

Patricia Grimble, Crowborough, East Sussex

Patricia, aged eight, with her beloved nan and granddad in 1950. The large lump in her cheek is Brighton rock!

Great gardening
Eucomis

One of the most inspiring countries to visit if you're a gardener is South Africa because the range of plants is awe-inspiring. One plant that also grows quite happily here is the pineapple flower, eucomis – so called because of the leafy bracts at the top of its stems. The species most commonly grown in the UK are E bicolor and E comosa, but the specialist nursery Broadleigh Gardens has introduced E van der merwei, which has unusually marked leaves that complement the flowers beautifully. Remember to bring them inside during winter.

■ To order, visit the website at www.broadleighbulbs.co.uk

My childhood home

Little Madeleine

O ur house was divided into two flats – Mum, Dad and I lived downstairs and the Triggs family upstairs. We shared an outside lavatory which meant they had to climb up and down an exposed iron staircase to use it.

The kitchen had an old range which had to be black-leaded. Without a bathroom, we washed in the scullery sink. For my nightly ablutions, I sat on the draining board with my feet in the sink, reciting my multiplication tables, supervised by my Dad, who would give me a reward as I learned each one. At the age of five, I could say my 12 times table and received sixpence – a fortune then.

Gas lit every room, and the day the gas meter man came was a bonus day, as he gave Mum some money back.

Lacking in comforts, we didn't feel underprivileged, just content with our lot. There was one thing we did have plenty of, though, and that was love.

Madeleine Croll, Tankerton, Kent

TOP TIP

Tea towels can be kept in excellent colour by putting the rind of a lemon in the water you wash them in.

S Smith, Coulsdon, Surrey

In the kitchen

LAMB AND THYME HOTPOT

Serves 3-4
- 450g (1 lb) lean lamb neck fillet, cut into thin medallions
- 1 onion, sliced
- 1 leek, sliced
- 1 carrot, sliced
- 300 ml (approx ½ pint) beer
- 150 ml stock (¼ pint)
- 1 tablespoon gravy granules
- 1 tablespoon fresh thyme, chopped
- 2 potatoes, peeled and thinly sliced
- 2 parsnips, peeled and thinly sliced
- Butter

1 In a non-stick pan, dry fry the lamb fillet with the onion, leek and carrot for 4-5 minutes until browned. Add the beer, stock, gravy granules and fresh thyme and cook for further 2-3 minutes until thickened.

2 Season with salt and pepper and transfer to an ovenproof casserole dish or individual ovenproof pots.

3 Cover the lamb with the sliced potatoes and parsnips and brush with a little melted butter. Cover with foil and cook in pre-heated oven at 180°C, 350°F or Gas Mark 4 for 1 hour. Uncover for the last 30 minutes to allow the potatoes and parsnips to brown. *Recipe courtesy www.meatmatters.com*

We remember when...

The two-tier post system was first introduced this week in 1968. The new 5d first class stamps meant that letters would be delivered overnight, while the four pence stamps had a slower service. At first the new system caused confusion with both business and the public, with many expressing their doubts but the system of first and second class post is still with us today.

Great gardening

Zelkova

Few gardeners have heard of a tree called zelkova, but it makes a majestic specimen with upswept branches and is loved for its amazing autumn colours. One of the newer cultivars is Z serrata 'Kiwi Sunset' which has a dainty, semi-weeping habit. However, what makes it really special are its lime green leaves which become golden during the summer. It's an excellent tree for a small garden, especially where a golden elm would be too large.
■ Order one from Notcutts Garden Centres or www.notcutts.co.uk

▓ AROUND THE HOUSE ▓

Be on the lookout now for 'Two for One' toiletry and gift offers in supermarkets, to spread the cost of Christmas presents.

Superfood!

▓ EAT MORE... APPLES ▓
Packed with...

Vitamin C, magnesium, pectin, calcium, phosphorus, phytonutrient quercitin and fructose.

Good for...

Giving your immunity system a boost, while helping to break down fats and reducing cholesterol. Also thought to help relieve indigestion and keep you regular too, as well as relieving the symptoms of inflammatory diseases, such as gout, rheumatism and arthritis.

Get more by...

Braising with red cabbage, grating on to breakfast cereal or serving with savoury crackers and slices of blue cheese.

A Grand Day Out

The highlight of my long summer holidays was a trip to my grandparents for lunch. I'd allow myself to be on the receiving end of hugs and kisses, then I'd dash off down the garden path to see my grandfather.

He was the local blacksmith and I spent many happy hours pumping the bellows for him, while he shod a large shire horse or made new wheels for a farmer's cart. I can remember the smell of the forge and how I stood wide-eyed when grandfather immersed the glowing hot iron holding the horse shoe into the large trough of murky water.

Lunchtime was unforgettable – grandmother would always serve pudding first, although I never knew why; the main course was usually pork which I always ate with relish. It was tinged with a certain amount of guilt as

I knew I was eating one of grandfather's hand-reared pigs. As I ate, I tried not to think about the times I'd stood talking to them, and scratching them behind the ears.

After lunch, the children would all settle down on the pegged rugs in front of the fire and grandmother would hand us the button boxes. She'd saved a wonderful collection and we'd sort through them.

All too soon, it was time to go, but not before grandmother took me to the granary and gave me some large cooking apples and lovely red eaters. Goodbyes said, I would pedal off into the sunset with the memory of another lovely day.
Doreen Bryan, Winchester, Hants

Doreen aged 14, in 1950

My childhood home

Barbara's house
in Hammerwich

I was adopted in 1943 and grew up hearing people in the village saying, 'That's the little girl the Jarvis's adopted'. Nevertheless, I had a happy childhood in Hammerwich, Staffordshire and the thing I recall about our house was we didn't have a bathroom.

Each Saturday night Dad would carry a large tin bath in and put it in front of the grate. Dad was a miner, so with the coal allowance, we had roaring fires. The water for my bath was heated in two kettles on the hob to boil.

I remember Dad sitting with the paper placed in front of him, so I had privacy.

We had an outside toilet which had two distinct smells. In the winter months, Dad would hang a paraffin lamp on the cistern to keep the pipes from freezing. The other smell was oranges. Mom used to buy large Jaffa oranges and keep the soft tissue they came wrapped in for use in the toilet – it was better than newspaper.

**Barbara Roberts,
Burntwood, Staffs**

Great gardening

Violas

Few bedding plants flower reliably all summer but violas are an exception. Natives of the northern hemisphere and related to the wild pansy, heartsease, there are hundreds of cultivars to choose between. New this year is the viola 'Brush Strokes'. An unusual variety, it produces flowers in a kaleidoscope of colour between March and November. Sow seed inside between February and April or outside from May onwards.
■ Seeds are available by calling 01638 751 161 or www.fothergills.co.uk

Superfood!

EAT MORE... BLACKBERRIES

Packed with...

Vitamins C and E, calcium, magnesium, pectin, potassium, phosphorus, fibre and folate, plus antioxidant anthocyanin.

Good for...

Helping the immune system fight infection and protecting the body from the effects of free radicals (toxic cells). Beneficial for the heart and circulatory system and are also thought to help lower cholesterol.

Get more by...

Sprinkling on to cereal and porridge or blend into a healthy smoothie with chunks of apple and spoons of low-fat yoghurt.

In the kitchen

PLUM AND FOREST FRUITS CRUMBLE

Serves 4-6
- 500 g (1 lb 2 oz) plums, quartered and stones removed
- 500 g (1 lb 2 oz) bag frozen forest fruits
- 100 g (3½ oz) golden caster sugar
- ½ teaspoon ground cinnamon

For the crumble
- 150 g (5 oz) plain wholemeal flour
- 125 g (4½ oz) chilled butter, cubed
- 100 g (3½ oz) oats
- 100 g (3½ oz) golden caster sugar

1 Preheat the oven to 190°C, 375°F or Gas Mark 5. Put the plums and forest fruits into the base of an ovenproof dish. Sprinkle with the golden caster sugar and cinnamon and gently mix together.

2 Put the flour into a bowl and add the butter. Rub together with your fingertips until the mixture resembles crumbs (or alternatively blend for a few seconds in a food processor).

3 Add the oats and sugar and stir together. Sprinkle over the fruit. Bake for 30 minutes until the fruit is tender and the crumble is cooked through.

Recipe courtesy Billington's and Allinson

We remember when...

A second television channel was launched this week in 1955. The BBC had been the only television channel for 18 years, and was concerned about competition from ITA (later known as ITV). The new channel would also show advertisements for the first time. The first programme on ITA was a variety show, with an advert break after the first hour. What a difference to today, where adverts seem to come round all the time!

A Grand Day Out

Valerie and her family at Bognor

This is a photograph of my sister and myself at Bognor in the 1940s with our parents. I am in the middle, my sister on my right beside my Mum, my Dad directly behind me.

We used to go in what my Dad called a charabanc, and the night before my Mum would get long strips of rag and wind our hair round it to make ringlets, and we had to sleep with them in.

The next morning we set off with beautiful curls but at the slightest hint of rain, they would drop out and we would be left with our usual straight hair! Everyone was so formal, dressed in their Sunday best and the dads in their suits, ties and best flat caps.

Some people took picnics but we always had fish and chips in a café, which we thought was lovely. Dad saved up so that we could play on the machines, a penny a go.

I loved it all so much I told my Mum that when I got older I was going to live in Bognor. It was a good thing that my husband loved it as much as I did, because when we retired we moved here!

**Valerie Swadling,
Bognor Regis, West Sussex**

AROUND THE HOUSE

If you have trouble threading a needle, spray a little hair lacquer on to the end of the cotton strand, which will stiffen it and make it much easier to thread.

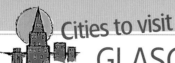

GLASGOW: ANCIENT AND MODERN

From P & O to Art Nouveau

Once renowned for shipbuilding, Glasgow is today more widely known as the home of Charles Rennie Mackintosh. Art Nouveau fans make a pilgrimage to the city solely to admire examples of his work such as the Willow Tea Rooms. On a grander scale, The Lighthouse is a centre for architecture and design housed in what used to be the Glasgow Herald newspaper office designed by Mackintosh in 1895. Take the lift to Level Six to enjoy stunning views across the city.

Situated on the banks of the River Clyde, Glasgow first grew to prosperity through trade with North America but the city's grey, heavy industry image was cast aside for good when it became European City of Culture in 1990 and the focus shifted to its remarkable museums and galleries – 20 in all.

Chief among these is GoMA (Gallery of Modern Art), one of the finest collections of contemporary art outside London. It is housed in a Grecian style mansion close to a famous Glasgow landmark, a statue of the Duke of Wellington.

Unique to Glasgow is the Burrell Collection, comprising over 9,000 artworks bequeathed by their collector Sir William Burrell in 1944. Works by Degas and Cezanne can be seen alongside medieval art, tapestries and English oak furniture in a modern building set in peaceful woodland.

Shoppers who love a secondhand bargain make their way to The Barras a covered flea market that owes its existence to Maggie McIver who, in the 1920s, used to rent out barrows to other market traders. Above the market was the Barrowland Ballroom which used to be a popular dancehall and is now a well-known venue for today's bands.

The bells rang out

Ruby Park of Saxmundham earned pocket money by helping on the farm

Our village

I was born in the small Suffolk village of Sternfield. My father, Ted Ayden, was a bricklayer and stonemason who was on the parish council for many years. He was always known as Ringer because he was the bell ringer for the church. There were four bells and Dad used to ring three of them, one with each hand and the other with his foot. My sister or I would ring the fourth one.

Our local shop was a small room in my aunt's house where she sold cigarettes, crisps, pop and the odd tin or packet of food. Most of our shopping was delivered from our nearest town, Saxmundham.

We did not have a village green but we had a meadow where we used to play all the usual games with other children. The farmer used to have his horses in the meadow for part of the year and our next-door neighbour kept pigs in the far corner.

A river at the bottom of our garden formed the boundary between Sternfield and the next village, Benhall. Just down the road there was a ford with a rickety old wooden bridge over it where we used to paddle and play and get ourselves soaking wet.

I was horse mad and from the age of twelve I used to help the farmer stack the sheaves as they came off the binder. Then when he collected them and put them into a stack I sat astride a large Suffolk Punch called Bess and kicked her down the rows. At the end of the day I would take off her tackle and lead her down to the pond for a drink. For this I was paid the princely sum of one shilling a week.

pic: rex features

Naughty Nineties

1 What age was John Major when he became Prime Minister?
A 49
B 46
C 47
D 45

2 Which of these films won the 1991 academy award for best picture?
A Silence Of The Lambs
B The Unforgiven
C JFK
D Bugsy

3 Which team won the 1992 FA Cup?
A Manchester United
B Liverpool
C Sunderland
D Wolverhampton

4 Boyzone (pictured) had their first hit with Love Me For A Reason. The song was previously a 70s hit for…?
A The Osmonds
B David Cassidy
C David Soul
D Smokey

5 When did the Church of England begin to ordain women priests?
A 1990
B 1994
C 1991
D 1992

6 Which veteran astronaut became the oldest space traveller in 1998?
A Buzz Aldrin
B Neil Armstrong
C John Glenn
D Michael Collins

7 In which US state is the fictional town of Twin Peaks?
A Washington
B Texas
C New York
D California

8 In which year was Hong Kong returned to China?
A 1994
B 1997
C 1999
D 1996

9 Who was the voice of Buzz Lightyear in Toy Story?
A Tom Hanks
B John Goodman
C Tim Allen
D Brendan Fraser

10 Who won the British Open Golf Championship in 1990?
A Seve Ballesteros
B Nick Faldo
C Ian Baker Finch
D Mark Calcavecchia

Answers: 1C, 2A, 3B, 4A, 5D, 6C, 7A, 8B, 9C, 10B

DRAGON IN DISGUISE

BY ANGELA SHEPHERD

Young Susan dreads starting school – and fears the headmistress even more

I was helping Nanna with the baking when the doorbell went. She was up to her elbows in flour so Auntie Marge had to put down her curling tongs and answer the door.

She came back holding a piece of paper, which she handed to me: "It's for our Susan. An invitation." I was just five years old so I gave it back to her and said: "You'll have to read it for me."

"Who was it?" inquired Nanna, pummelling the bread dough.

"It was The Dragon," replied Auntie Marge. Putting on an important voice, she read: "Miss H. Hodgkiss invites Miss Susan Appleton for tea at the School House on Sunday at four o'clock. RSVP."

I didn't like the sound of this at all. Miss Hodgkiss had been headmistress of the village school for years. She had taught Auntie Marge who always called her The Dragon. 'Eyes in the back of her head, she had', according to Auntie Marge, 'and a tongue sharp enough to slice bacon'.

Starting school in September wasn't a happy prospect for me. I could see the playground from my bedroom window. At playtime, Miss Hodgkiss patrolled, tall and thin, carrying her cup of tea, keeping an eagle eye on everything.

Last week Mam and I had taken her a punnet of rosehips we'd gathered. The schoolchildren were collecting them to be made into rosehip syrup for babies. Miss Hodgkiss had given me a badge with a rosehip on it and Mam said

There was a lead weight in my chest as I trailed round

it was because I had helped with the war effort.

"Well, now, you are honoured, Susan," said Nanna, putting a cloth over the bread dough, "That will be because of all those rosehips you picked. We'll have to send a note back. That's what RSVP means."

"I don't want to go," I said.

I had to wait till tea-time to find out what Mam thought because she was working at the Post Office, helping Uncle Tom, Nanna's brother who also had a smallholding nearby.

When Mam came in she said that it would be rude to refuse. Granddad tried to cheer me up. "Take no notice of our Marge," he said, puffing on his after-tea pipe, "Miss Hodgkiss is a nice lady. She was a good-looking lass when she was young; it's not her fault she's on the shelf. I'll walk round with you on Sunday."

I resigned myself to my fate, but there was a lead weight in my chest as I trailed round to the School House with Granddad. Mam had buttoned me into my best Fair Isle cardigan and put my hair in bunches. We went to the back door and I was handed over. Miss Hodgkiss told Granddad she would bring me home after tea.

My heart was thumping but it wasn't so bad, after all. Miss Hodgkiss showed me the classrooms. I saw pictures on the walls and the books the children used. Miss Hodgkiss let me choose one to look at while she prepared the tea.

We were in the kitchen when there was a knock at the door. It was my Uncle Tom, carrying a basket with some apples and two brown eggs. He took off his cap and waved at me over Miss Hodgkiss's shoulder, his face ruddy and smiley, like always.

"Now then, Hilary, I thought you and young Susan might like these eggs for tea." He wouldn't come in, saying he had the milking to do.

Miss Hodgkiss boiled the eggs and we had bread soldiers with them, then she walked me home.

Nanna was washing up. Auntie Marge was drying and Mam was putting away. Granddad was packing his bag ready for his shift at the Observer Corps hut. When they asked me what had happened, I said: "She was nice, and I don't mind about going to school, now."

"I'll help you write a thank you note," said Mam. When we'd finished, I asked: "How do I write 'Miss H Hodgkiss'?"

"What do you think the H stands for?" wondered Auntie Marge.

"Hilda?" suggested Mam.

"Could be Honoria," Nanna said. "When I was in service, one of the daughters was called Honoria."

'I don't mind about going to school'

I stopped chewing the end of my pencil. "Her name is Hilary," I told them.

Everyone stared at me. Nanna looked at me over the top of her glasses: "And how come you know such a thing, young lady?"

"She's making it up," laughed Auntie Marge.

"No, I'm not! Uncle Tom called her Hilary when he brought the eggs for our tea."

"Did he now?" Nanna sounded quite put out. "Well, our Tom's a dark horse and no mistake. Eggs for tea! And first names!"

Mam said: "Miss Hodgkiss is in the chapel choir and Uncle Tom's been playing the organ since Sally Robinson joined the ATS."

"What do you make of it, John?" Nanna addressed Granddad.

Granddad paused on his way out: "It's a match," he said.

I thought he was talking about the Swan Vesta he was lighting his pipe with. I understood better when they dressed me in salmon-pink satin for the wedding and Miss Hodgkiss turned into Auntie Hilary (but only out of school).

A tiny little thing like a name and Granddad knew straightaway what was going to happen. He turned out to be right. But then Granddad always was.

October 2008

Wednesday
1

Thursday
2

Friday
3

Saturday
4

Sunday
5

Monday
6

Tuesday
7
Yours magazine on sale

Wednesday
8
Horse of the Year Show begins

Thursday
9

Friday
10

Saturday
11

Sunday
12

Monday
13

Tuesday
14

Wednesday
15

Thursday
16

Friday
17

Saturday
18

Sunday
19

Monday
20

Tuesday
21
Yours magazine on sale

Wednesday
22

Thursday

23

Friday

24
United Nations' Day

Saturday

25

Sunday

26
British Summer Time (BST) ends. Clocks go back

Monday

27

Tuesday

28

Wednesday

29

Thursday

30

Friday

31
Hallowe'en

PIC: REX FEATURES

Born this month

Academy award-winning actress and singer Julie Andrews (pictured) was born on October 1, 1935, in Walton-on-Thames, Surrey. She starred in the Broadway musical My Fair Lady and in film classics The Sound of Music and Mary Poppins.

Married this month

Sixties pop duo Sonny and Cher married on October 27, 1964. They'd first met in a Los Angeles coffee shop two years earlier and had a string of chart-topping hits together in the 1960s.

Died this month

Actor and film maker Orson Welles died of a heart attack on October 10 1985, at the age of 70. Famous for his radio broadcast of The War of The Worlds, based on the book by H G Wells, the reading panicked thousands across America who tuned in late and believed the world was under attack from Martians.

My childhood home

TOP TIP
To avoid losing buttons on new clothes, dab the centre threads of each button with clear nail varnish.

Fran Pickering, Kendal, Cumbria

The house where I was born in Lancashire was also where my Mum was born and where my great-grandma lived. Sadly, my grandma died in childbirth when my Mum was born, so my great-grandma brought her up, because granddad had to work. It was a two-up, two-down terrace and, so I've been told, was originally built as a pub but was never opened as one. Next door was made into a grocers and pie shop.

The front room had a piano and there was a treadle sewing machine in one corner, and a cupboard with a mesh front where my mum kept the cod liver oil.

Ann's childhood home

When I married, we bought the house next door on the other side to the shop. My parents both died in 2003, and I knew I couldn't sell the house where I was born, so I sold mine and moved back into the old house.

I know I've made the right decision and I feel my parents and great-grandma are still with me, looking after me.

Ann Symington, Lancashire

Great gardening

Fittonias

Although fittonias have been used as houseplants for many years they've never really received the attention they deserve. Their unusually marked leaves are highly decorative and look great against a plain background. They can be a little tricky, requiring high levels of humidity but it's worth persevering with them. As spreading evergreen perennials from South America, they do best when grown among other houseplants or in a terrarium.

■ You can buy them at most large garden centres, or for more details visit www.flowers.org

Superfood!
EAT MORE... FIGS
Packed with...

Vitamin C, potassium, magnesium, phosphorus, calcium and beta-carotene.

Good for...

Increasing vitality, clearing toxins from the body and helping to move sluggish bowels.

Get more by...

Splitting into quarters and baking with wedges of goat's cheese and freshly ground pepper. Serve on a bed of lettuce.

■ AROUND THE HOUSE

Now's the time to have your electric blanket serviced. It needs to be done by the manufacturer, and every three years at least. If you haven't run your central heating yet, give it a dummy run to see if all is running well.

In the kitchen

■ MANGO AND PASSIONFRUIT TRIFLE ■

Serves 8
- 150 g (5 oz) packet ratafia or amaretti biscuits
- 150 ml (¼ pint) rum or sherry
- 1 mango, peeled and sliced
- 1 papaya, peeled, halved, seeds removed and sliced
- Juice of ½ lime
- 1 small pineapple, peeled and cut into quarters, woody core removed
- 500 g (1 lb 2 oz) carton fresh vanilla custard

For the topping
- 200 g (7 oz) mascarpone
- 284 ml (approx ½ pint) carton double cream, softly whipped
- Finely grated zest of ½ lime
- ¼ teaspoon vanilla extract
- 50 g (2 oz) unrefined dark muscovado sugar

1 Put the biscuits in the base of 8 glasses and drizzle over some of the rum or sherry.
2 Scatter some mango, papaya, lime juice and pineapple pieces into each glass. Pour over the rest of the rum or sherry. Pour the custard over the fruit.
3 Mix together the mascarpone, double cream, lime zest and vanilla extract. Spoon on top of the custard and sprinkle with the dark muscovado sugar.

Recipe courtesy Billington's

We remember when...

The Festival of Britain drew to an end this week in September 1951. The festival celebrated British art, architecture, science and industry. It also aimed to raise spirits after the austere war years and give inspiration and ideas for rebuilding the buildings ruined by war throughout the country. The main exhibitions were on the South Bank of the Thames, but many communities took part in the celebrations countrywide.

A Grand Day Out

Left: Marion's Mum and Dad, and sister Dorothy in Hunstanton, 1954
Above Marion, her Dad and Dorothy at Clacton

This is a picture of my Mother, Father and sister on holiday in Hunstanton in 1954. Notice Mother has her knitting – she took it everywhere. It was a boiling hot day but Dad has got his pullover on. Normally he'd wear his cap but he put my hat on instead to pose for the photo! I'm not in the picture as I'd received a Brownie camera for my birthday and wouldn't let anyone touch it.

The other photo is of Dad, me (with the pigtails) and my sister Dorothy in Clacton, the day of the Godmanchester Union Chapel Sunday School outing.

Just as on the beach, Dad was fully dressed in jumper and all; we're wearing our cardigans and Dad is carrying our coats 'just in case'.

With us were my grandmother and aunty. Grandma was lovely and loved sweets and ice cream, so a day out with her was full of treats. This was just after the war and we couldn't buy ice creams in our small towns, and sweets were rationed, so grandma and granddad used to give us theirs (although grandma usually came with us to buy them and ate as many as we did!)

Not all the beach was open either because of the fear of land mines in the sand, so we were restricted as to where we could build sandcastles or paddle, but it was all great fun.

Marion Newman, Raunds, Northampton

In the kitchen

CHOP SUEY

Serves 2
- 5 ml (1 teaspoon) oil
- 2 garlic cloves, crushed
- 2.5 cm (1 in) root ginger, peeled and thinly sliced
- 225 g (8 oz) lean beef, lamb or pork grilling/ frying steaks, cut into thin strips
- 1 carrot, peeled and cut into thin strips
- 100 g (approx 4 oz) pak choi, chinese leaf or cabbage, shredded
- 300 g (10 ½ oz) beansprouts
- 30 ml (2 tablespoons) soy sauce
- 45 ml (3 tablespoons) plum sauce
- 15 ml (1 tablespoon) tomato ketchup

1 In a large non-stick wok or saucepan, heat the oil and fry the garlic and root ginger for 1-2 minutes.

2 Add the beef, lamb or pork strips and cook for 2-3 minutes, or until browned. Add the carrot strips and cook for 1-2 minutes.

3 Add the pak choi, Chinese leaf or cabbage, the beansprouts, soy sauce, plum sauce and tomato ketchup. Cook for 1-2 minutes.

Recipe courtesy www.meatmatters.com

TOP TIP

If you have an electric cooker with solid rings, put a pan of cold water on the ring after you finish cooking. The retained heat will heat the water for you to use to wash your dishes.

Mrs D Mealor, St Helens, Merseyside

My childhood home

Edna's mum in the kitchen in 1968, the 'climbing in' window behind!

I was born in May 1942 in the front bedroom of 5 Hill Road, Leyland, Lancashire, and lived there with my brothers Sydney and Gordon.

Mum and Dad rented it from a private landlord and I remember that in the 1950s, the rent was 9/6d a week, including the council rates.

We had a small lounge with a farmhouse range for heating and water. On Saturday nights the family would listen to the radio which worked off an accumulator. Often Mum would put potatoes and onions under the grate with the ashes, to cook for our supper.

Us children helped around the house and it was our job to collect the branches that had fallen in Bluebell Wood, to keep the fire going.

In our back garden we grew soft fruit, lettuce and salad vegetables and we kept 14 dandy hens in a pen. Next door

Edna's home

had hens that run loose and they had a habit of coming through our front door, running up the stairs and laying an egg on the landing, then running out again. My Mother, who was very honest would return it next door.

Our kitchen was very small but there was always a good smell of pies and cakes coming from it, and if Mum had time, she baked bread as well. If Gordon and I arrived home from school before Mum, I'd climb through the kitchen window, unlock the back door and let my brother in. We'd raid the bread bin, then nip out the front door so Mum wouldn't know we'd been in.

Edna Lydiate, Lancs

We remember when...

Elizabeth Taylor and Richard Burton secretly remarried this week in 1975, only 17 months after their divorce. They'd first married in 1964, after falling in love when they filmed Cleopatra in Rome, but split up after ten years. Second time round, they had a simple wedding in Africa and spent their honeymoon on safari in Botswana.

Superfood!

EAT MORE... SWEETCORN

Packed with...

Potassium, iron, calcium, dietary fibre, vitamins B3, A and C, magnesium and zinc.

Good for...

Maintaining a healthy brain and nervous system. Plus, may help reduce the symptoms of eczema.

Get more by...

Boiling, grilling, or barbecuing whole – serve with a slice of lemon and freshly ground pepper. Add the kernels to curries, stews, stir-fries, fritters, pasta dishes and salads.

AROUND THE HOUSE

If you've got scuff or water marks on wooden furniture, cut a brazil nut in half, and rub the raw edge gently into the stain, along the grain of the wood.

Great gardening

Chiritas

Chiritas are a little-known group of plants, but are well worth discovering. They come mainly from Sri Lanka, India and Southeast Asia and are grown for their unusual yet attractive leaves, which are often covered in intricate silver designs. Others are grown for their trumpet-shaped lavender, yellow or white flowers. Since most require relatively warm temperatures, and moderate levels of humidity, they thrive in a well-lit bathroom (avoid direct sunlight). However, you're unlikely to find them at garden centres, so may need to try a specialist nursery such as Dibleys instead.

■ You can learn more about these plants by visiting www.dibleys.com

A Grand Day Out

In 1952, when I was 16, my friend Thelma and I spent the day at Wicksteed Park in Kettering. It was a favourite place, close to Market Harborough where I grew up.

I was wearing my new outfit, grey skirt and grey houndstooth jacket with matching chiffon scarf – Thelma and I thought we were very smart. Nowadays, it's jeans and a T-shirt.

The second photograph is of me 45 years later in Market Harborough, taken by my same friend, Thelma. We had a nostalgic reunion, remembering the good old days at Welland Park Secondary School, the teachers, especially our headmaster, Mr Winterbottom, who we all nicknamed 'Summertop'. Cheeky, weren't we?

Cynthia Tebbutt, Market Harborough

Fashionable Cynthia at Wicksteed Park
Inset: Cynthia during that nostalgic reunion

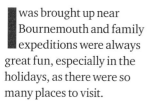

A Grand Day Out

I was brought up near Bournemouth and family expeditions were always great fun, especially in the holidays, as there were so many places to visit.

My favourite days out were spent in the New Forest or on the water. Sometimes my father would take us deer and badger watching, and we would happily sit for hours in one of the watching towers until we were rewarded by the sight of a doe and her fawn, or badgers coming out to play at dusk.

My father also taught us to paddle a canoe, and that was always a great day out. Sometimes we canoed along the coast, but there was always the risk of being swept out to sea; so generally we kept to the harbours and rivers.

Keyhaven, with its maze of channels and its birdlife was my favourite canoeing place. We got cold, wet and muddy, of course, but that was part of the fun.

We usually seemed to be boating, walking or watching wildlife, which is probably why I'm still happiest out of doors.

**Christine Barrett,
Bournemouth**

Canoeing at Keyhaven in 1962

We remember when...

The new seven-sided 50p coin was issued this week in 1969, to replace ten shilling notes. It was the third decimal coin to be introduced in Britain but many people felt it was too similar to the new ten pence piece, which was introduced in April. There were still three new coins to come, the 2p, 1p and the half pence, which were introduced on Decimal Day in February 1971.

In the kitchen
■ BLUEBERRY SCONES ■
Makes 8

- ■ 250 g (9 oz) white self-raising flour
- ■ 1 teaspoon baking powder
- ■ 25 g (1 oz) unrefined golden caster sugar
- ■ 50 g (2 oz) chilled butter, diced
- ■ 50 g (2 oz) dried blueberries
- ■ 284 ml (approx ¹/₂ pint) carton buttermilk

To serve
- ■ 100 g (approx 4 oz) mascarpone cheese
- ■ 4 tablespoons Greek yoghurt
- ■ 2 tablespoons unrefined golden caster sugar
- ■ ¹/₄ teaspoon vanilla extract
- ■ 8 tablespoons blueberry jam

1 Put an ungreased baking sheet into the oven and pre-heat the oven to 230°C, 450°F or Gas Mark 8.
2 Sift flour and baking powder together and add the golden caster sugar.
3 Add butter and rub together to make crumbs. Add blueberries and pour in buttermilk and mix.
4 Knead dough lightly on floured surface and roll out to a thickness of 2.5 cm (1 in).
5 Use a 5 cm (2 in) plain pastry cutter to stamp out 8 rounds of dough. Lift scones on to pre-heated baking sheet. Bake for 12-15 minutes until pale golden.
6 For the filling, mix together mascarpone cheese, Greek yoghurt, golden caster sugar and vanilla extract.
7 To serve, split scones in half and serve with dollop of mascarpone mixture and blueberry jam.

Recipe courtesy Billington's and Allinson

Great gardening

Calatheas

Natives of tropical South America, calatheas thrive in softly lit, warm, highly humid places, so need a shady corner in a heated conservatory if they're going to grow happily in this country. Although the flowers of many calatheas are quite insignificant, all make great houseplants (if given the correct conditions) because their architectural intricately marked leaves are a joy to behold. And the best is Calathea crocata because it not only boasts ornate foliage but scorching orange flowers.

■ Available from larger garden centres, visit The Flowers and Plants Association at www.flowers.org.uk to learn more.

AROUND THE HOUSE

To clean flowerpots, use washing up liquid and hot water and scrub with a stiff brush to remove deposits, bacteria and algae. Rinse with a solution of 10 parts water to 1 part bleach, then rinse with cold water and leave to dry.

Superfood!

EAT MORE... SOYA BEANS

Packed with...

Protein, iron, calcium, phosphorus, beta-carotene, amino acids, vitamins B3 and C, plus omega-3 essential fatty acids.

Good for...

Lowering cholesterol. This potent phyto-oestrogen may also prevent breast and ovarian cancers.

Get more by...

Adding to casseroles, stews and soups. Can also be added to spaghetti bolognaise, chillies and curries.

TOP TIP

If you're going away on a break, put leftover milk in ice cube trays and freeze. One or two cubes melt quickly for a cup of tea on your return home.   **Mrs H Wright, Southampton**

My childhood home

I was five weeks old when my parents and nine-year-old brother moved into a newly built house on a council estate in Sheffield – 136 Hallowmoor Road, in the 1930s Sadly, my brother, Ronald, died five years later.

We didn't have carpets and every autumn Mum and I made a new pegged rug from strips of old coats and material, ready for winter. If we were cold in bed, we pulled on coats and warmed our feet on hot oven shelves from the coal oven, wrapped in an old blanket – bliss!

The annual Fair (Wadsley Feast) would arrive, the big lorries and trucks full of roundabouts and stalls, and I would lie in bed watching the headlights slowly travel round the bedroom as they made their way to set up.

The field behind No 136 was my reading room. I would hide in the grass, ignoring Mother's calls until I had finished the chapter.

I lost my special place to the RAF and the Army when the war years came. As we headed for our air raid shelters, I could hear the rustle of the guards' coats as they patrolled the perimeter. The soldiers bought me a box of chocolates for my birthday – I'd be about nine years old.

Jean Lockwood, Sheffield

Jean and brother Ronald outside No 136, around 1934

Great gardening
African violet

If there's one plant gardeners rarely get excited about, it's the African violet. Perhaps they associate it with dusty windowsills and maiden aunts, but that's not really fair. Saintpaulias, as they're botanically known, hail from mountainous regions of South Africa and make great little plants, thriving on neglect while flowering almost continuously. They're widely available from garden centres, but if you want to try a new variety, visit a specialist nursery such as Dibleys at www.dibleys.com.

■ Tip – the plants may rot if the leaves get wet so pour water into the saucer rather than the container

A Grand Day Out

Ian, aged 16, in 1938

We couldn't afford a summer holiday in 1938 but spent our holiday instead at the Empire Exhibition at Bellahouston Park in Glasgow. It was opened on May 4 by King George VI and Queen Elizabeth, and closed at the end of October, by which time it had been visited by 13.5 million people.

The Exhibition was built on 175 acres at Bellahouston Park and was visited by Queen Mary and the Dukes and Duchesses of Kent and Gloucester.

'We three' also went – myself (Ian, aged 16) brother Kenneth, 12, and sister Edna, who was 10 – and were so excited. We all had season tickets for the summer, with a blue cover and a red Exhibition lion on the front, costing 12s 6d.

We had a wonderful time visiting the fascinating buildings and pavilions, like a mysterious fairyland, topped by Thomas Tait's 300ft Tower of Empire.

Ian Cormack, Glasgow

Superfood!
EAT MORE... BANANAS

Packed with...

Vitamins B6, C and K, potassium, fibre, manganese, zinc, iron, folic acid, calcium and tryphophan.

Good for...

Enhancing mood, improving brain function and promoting strong, healthy muscles, including the heart. Can also help reduce blood pressure and aid digestion, preventing heartburn.

Get more by...

Adding to oatmeal or porridge with a spoon of maple syrup or honey. Alternatively, slice and mix with peanut butter for a nutritious sandwich filling.

In the kitchen

■ BUTTERED SWEDE WITH CRISPY BACON ■

Serves 4

- ■ 1 small to medium-sized swede, about 700 g (1½ lb)
- ■ Salt and coarsely ground black pepper
- ■ 4 rashers smoked streaky bacon
- ■ Small bunch fresh chives (optional)
- ■ 50 g (2 oz) butter

1 Peel the swede and cut into large chunks. Drop into a pan of boiling, lightly-salted water and cook, uncovered, for 15-20 minutes or until very tender.

2 While the swede is cooking, grill the bacon until all the fat is very crisp. Leave to cool a little then chop quite roughly. Roughly chop the chives if using.

3 Drain the swede and mash with the butter and pepper until almost smooth. Pour in any bacon fat from the grill pan. Serve straight away with a little of the crispy bacon and chives sprinkled on top.

Recipe courtesy www.thinkvegetables.co.uk

■ AROUND THE HOUSE ■

Put a sheet of aluminium foil behind each radiator which will reflect back the heat into the room. And tuck your curtains behind the radiator – they'll still keep out the draughts.

We remember when...

The United Nations was born in 1945, at the end of the Second World War. It was hoped that an international organisation could help prevent another worldwide war in the future. Today the United Nations is made up of many parts, such as the World Health Organisation, International Monetary Fund and the World Bank, and more than 191 countries are members.

My childhood home

4 Vine Cottages, Anne's home on the right

I was born in February 1914 at 4 Vine Cottages, Epping. It was on the edge of Epping Forest, and I spent many happy childhood days playing there, building dens, climbing trees and making our own fun.

The common, too, was our playground, and in the summer holidays we spent our time helping with the haymaking on my uncle's farm, and after school we'd walk to the farm for milk and butter from the dairy. Most days, though, Henry delivered the milk by pony and trap, with his pint metal measures to pour straight into jugs.

Our cottage had three bedrooms, two sitting rooms, a front parlour, a middle kitchen with a large range, a passage to the scullery, with a stone copper to heat water for washing and bathing in a tin tub by the fire.

Mother was a good cook, even if money was tight; Dad kept rabbits and chickens and these helped out. Mum did sewing – boys' trousers and girls' shirts, and Dad grew vegetables on his allotment.

Times were quite hard but we were all so happy with our lives in those days.

**Anne Clarke,
Romford, Essex**

Anne, aged 4, in 1918

In the kitchen

▌ LOWER FAT FRESH FRUIT GATEAU ▌

Serves 10
- ■ 4 medium eggs
- ■ 125g (4½oz) caster sugar
- ■ Few drops vanilla essence
- ■ 125g (4½oz) plain flour
- ■ 4 tablespoons reduced-sugar raspberry jam
- ■ 6 tablespoons half-fat crème frâiche or whipped half-fat cream
- ■ 450g (1lb) assorted fresh fruit such as strawberries, raspberries, redcurrants, blueberries
- ■ 1 tablespoon icing sugar

1 Preheat oven to 190°C, 375°F, or Gas Mark 5. Grease and line two 20cm (8in) sandwich tins. Put the eggs and sugar in a large bowl over a pan of hot water. Whisk using an electric hand whisk until the mixture has doubled in volume and leaves a trail in the surface of the batter when the whisk is lifted.

3 Remove from the heat, stir in the vanilla essence and whisk for another 5 minutes until cooled. Sift half the flour over the mixture and fold in lightly using a large metal spoon. Sift and fold in the remaining flour. Pour into the prepared tins and spread evenly. Bake for 15 minutes until the cakes have risen and are firm to the touch. Turn out and cool on a wire rack.

4 When the cakes are cold, spread one with the jam and put on a serving plate. Top with fruit then spoon over the crème frâiche or cream alternative before sandwiching the two halves together. Sprinkle with icing sugar and chill until ready to serve.

Recipe courtesy Lion Quality Eggs

My childhood home

No 1 Buttercup Cottages

I was born in the end cottage of three in a village just in Sussex, which backed on to fields. My parents rented the cottage when they were married. I had a very happy childhood and went to the village school where I met my husband-to-be, Brian, when we were both eight years old.

We had no hot water and fetched all our water from a pump which was in the garden of No 3, the toilet in the garden of No 2.

My friends and I used to play in the field after school; my Father made two wickets and bats to play stoolball – children came to the back door asking Mother if my Father could come out to play!

I started going out with Brian when I was 21, and the next year my mother died. It was then that his parents moved away, so he moved in with my father and me, as our lodger. We married, and I think I can say that our children had as happy a childhood here in the cottage as I did.

I'm now 72 and the longest I've spent away from our cottage is 16 days, when we went on holiday. I can't see myself moving from here now, and have no wish to – of course, we now have water and all mod-cons laid on!

**Janet Groombridge,
Tunbridge Wells**

We remember when...

This week in 1957 the British government announced that life peerages would be introduced to the House of Lords and that women would be admitted for the first time. The first woman member of the House of Lords was Baroness Wootton of Abinger, a sociology professor and magistrate who was created a life peer in 1958.

▌ TOP TIP ▌

If you have a holiday caravan that has to be closed up for the winter, place large bowls of salt in the rooms when you leave. The salt will draw the moisture and will keep the inside of the van dry. **Pat Rolfe, Elm Park, Essex**

Superfood!

EAT MORE... PUMPKIN

Packed with...

Vitamin C, beta-carotene, potassium, magnesium, calcium and phosphorus.

Good for...

Maintaining a healthy liver and blood.

Get more by...

Scooping out the flesh to make a warming pumpkin stew or cut the flesh into fine strips, coat in egg and flour and fry in a little olive oil. Don't forget to make a Hallowe'en lantern from your pumpkin skin!

AROUND THE HOUSE

If you want to save your dinner service from chips and scratches, put a double thickness of kitchen towel between each plate when you stack them in the cupboard.

Great gardening

Aechmeas

Aechmeas originate in South America and, like many bromeliads, have such unusual blooms they make spectacular houseplants. At one time the most popular variety was 'Morgana', which is lovely except for the spikes on its leaves! However, after years of cross breeding, selection and multiplication a worthy successor, 'Primera', with smooth leaves and a larger flower was created. Like all bromeliads, the original plant dies off after flowering, but new shoots are soon produced. Aechmeas thrive when planted in a small container and enjoy a warm, light position, out of the sun. Water into the rosette during the summer, but avoid doing so when it's resting.

A Grand Day Out

A treat for my sister, Margaret, and me during school holidays in the late 1940s was an outing with Mum to Great Aunt Daisy at Beare Green.

We journeyed by two buses from Beckenham to Croydon, the Green Line bus to Holmwood, then a walk to 'Biddyfold', the homely red-brick bungalow self-built by Great Aunt Daisy's husband and brother, when bombed out of Stratford, London

With her menfolk at work, our company was welcomed by this wise and good-hearted East-Ender, invariably with the words, 'There, I dropped a spoon yesterday and knew Hilda and the girls would come'.

We loved picnicking in the large garden, collecting the newly-laid hens' eggs and side-stepping the strutting geese. Such happy, innocent days.

Our visits continued into adulthood, then with the luxury of a car, until Great Aunt Daisy sadly died in 1982.

**Janet Lambert,
Longfield, Kent**

Above: 'Biddyfold'
Below: Great Aunt Daisy (right), Janet's mum, Hilda (centre) and her Auntie Mabel

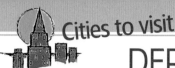
DERBY: ANCIENT AND MODERN

Silk and fine china

The Cathedral Quarter makes a great starting point for an exploration of Derby. Dominated by the cathedral's tall Perpendicular tower, the area boasts architecture from every period of history including one of the city's oldest surviving pubs, the Old Dolphin Inn in Queen Street.

With plenty of cafés and wine bars for refreshment breaks, the Quarter is a great place to shop with a variety of independent retailers, chief of which is Derby's own department store, Bennetts.

Derby played an important role in the birth of the Industrial Revolution when the first water-powered silk mill was opened in 1717. The original mill was destroyed by fire but its replacement, a Grade II listed building, now houses Derby's Museum of Industry and History. The city was equally famed for its china and you can still see it being made at the Royal Crown Derby Visitor Centre where there is also a museum and a shop.

More local porcelain can be seen in Derby Museum and Art Gallery which also has a fine collection of oil paintings by Joseph Wright. Born in Derby in 1734, he has been described as the first painter to express the spirit of the Industrial Revolution.

In recent times, Rolls Royce has been one of the biggest employers in Derby and the company's engineering centre is one of the city's most distinguished modern buildings. The statue of Henry Royce in the grounds originally stood in the Arboretum, which was first created in 1840 and is thought to be the first specially designed urban park in Britain.

Harvest home

Doreen Knowles of Bolton, Lancs, recalls the grand Noncomformist tradition of hymn singing

Our village

My village memories revolve around our Methodist chapel in a small village near Bolton. A large cotton mill and a steel works provided employment, as did a stone quarry, a bleachworks and a small bakery. When the local public house brewed its own beer, the whole village was engulfed in the awful aroma.

Harvest Festival was one of the highlights of the church year when it was bedecked with flowers and fruit and filled with relatives and friends. Each child recited a poem and I remember reciting, 'A little field mouse, soft as silk, a cow that gives us daily milk'.

After the service, bags of fruit and vegetables were sent out to the sick and aged. On the following Monday, we were able to buy bags of mixed fruit for three pennies. It was a rare treat to have grapes, even just four or five of them, when we were not ill.

Another special day was the annual 'Sermons' or Sunday School anniversary day which I have since learned were peculiar to the North of England. Old scholars from all over the country returned to attend the services. The chapel was full to overflowing with people standing in the aisles and, in true Methodist tradition, singing to lift the roof off.

I was in the Little Singers, a group of girls – all in white dresses – who stood on a platform at the front. I loved to sing and was chosen to sing solo on many occasions.

Later, I joined the Girls' Life Brigade. We met once a week to play games and learn crafts. We paid six old pence each week to buy our uniforms.

2000 and beyond...

1 What was the Labour majority after winning their second general election in 2001?
A 167 seats
B 157 seats
C 160 seats
D 125 seats

2 Where was David Beckham (right) born?
A Brixton
B Forest Hill
C Leytonstone
D Hendon

3 With her 2006 appearance in the relaunched Dr Who, Sarah Jane Smith has now assisted three Doctors. Which ones?
A Jon Pertwee, Christopher Eccleston, Tom Baker
B Tom Baker, Patrick Troughton, Christopher Eccleston
C David Tennant, Tom Baker, Peter Davison
D Tom Baker, Jon Pertwee, David Tennant

4 Who became the 'highest grossing' actor of all time in 2006?
A Tom Hanks
B Jack Nicholson
C Tom Cruise
D Kevin Costner

5 Which famous rock star did Johnny Depp claim to be the inspiration for his Pirates Of The Caribbean character, Captain Jack Sparrow?
A Mick Jagger
B David Bowie
C Roger Daltrey
D Keith Richards

6 2006 saw the re-make of Casino Royal. Who played Bond in the original?
A Peter O'Tool
B Woody Allen
C David Niven
D Peter Sellers

7 Who won the UK Snooker Championship in 2006?
A Stephen Hendry
B Peter Ebdon
C Ken Doherty
D Matthew Williams

8 Which famous director directed the CSI season five finale?
A Quentin Tarantino
B Oliver Stone
C Martin Scorsese
D Tim Burton

9 Which former Duran Duran member co-wrote material for Robbie William's 2005 album 'Intensive Care'?
A Simon LeBon
B Andy Taylor
C Stephen Duffy
D Nick Rhodes

10 Who was the voice of Sully in Monsters Inc?
A John Goodman
B Tom Hanks
C Billy Crystal
D Kevin Spacey

Answers: 1 A, 2 C, 3 D, 4 A, 5 D, 6 C, 7 B, 8 A, 9 C, 10 A

It's what I've always wanted

There wasn't much money for Christmas presents in the 1940s but Pam Clatworthy received a gift she's never forgotten

As children, we didn't realise that our lives were so impoverished. Christmas 1944 should have been a miserable time, for fancy food was scarce, many fathers were still away at war and the weather was extremely cold. Our parents, however, were determined that we should have a traditional Christmas and did their best to make it a good time for us.

On Christmas Day we sat around the glowing fire in the sitting-room opening our stockings. There wasn't a lot in them but, as a ten year old, I was delighted with a copy of my favourite girl's annual, The Girls Crystal. It had lots of exciting adventures involving spies in boarding schools and intrepid girl detectives who saw signals from enemy submarines far out at sea and alerted the authorities just in time. Gripping stuff!

I also had a dressing-gown made from an old grey car rug. The collar and cuffs were contrasting blue velvet salvaged from my Aunty Sylvia's going away wedding outfit. I paraded around the house just knowing that I looked like an American film star.

While this was going on, my sister was cycling round and round the old kitchen table, for in her stocking was a note from Father Christmas written in green ink which told her to look in the pantry for her present. This was a second-hand bicycle and she was allowed to use it indoors – kitchen only – as a Christmas treat.

But the best present of the season was the heavy snow. We hadn't really noticed it in the excitement of opening

The best present of the season was the heavy snow

our stockings but the strange translucence that only comes in snowy weather soon attracted our attention. It must have snowed for hours overnight, for when I looked out of the window the

Pam as a rather pensive 12 year old – dreaming of Christmas surprises, perhaps?

village street was covered in fluffy drifts that were as high as our garden hedge.

Best of all, was the number 31 bus that had got stuck in a drift, and there it was, right outside our garden gate, a bright red, double decker bus up to its axle in snow! The driver had obviously abandoned his vehicle and walked home the previous evening.

Discarding the glamorous dressing-gown, I rushed to put on my woollen socks, knitted woollen skirt and jumper and overcoat. My hand-knitted scarf, pixie hat and gloves and Wellington boots completed the outfit.

I planned the whole of the next enchanted day

my annual by the roaring fire. Meanwhile, my sister continued her endless cycling tour around the kitchen table.

On my way to bed I peered out of my bedroom window through the thick blackout curtains for a last look. Yes, it hadn't been a dream for there was our red bus shining magically in the bright moonlight.

"Good," I said to my Mother. "We'll have another day on the bus tomorrow." With my feet resting on the old, stone hot water bottle, and head under the eiderdown, I planned the whole of the next enchanted day.

Alas, during the night, a strong howling wind blew down our street and cold, clinging rain came in from the Bristol Channel. By the time I woke up on Boxing Day, all the snow had disappeared and the bus had been driven back to its depot.

It was hard to get over my disappointment but children are resilient, I put on my posh new dressing-gown and paraded downstairs. My sister had progressed from cycling around the kitchen table and was now wobbling up and down the slushy village street on her bike being cheered on by our Dad.

I picked up my girl's annual and curled up on the comfy chair. Christmas had been great, the presents appreciated, but best of all was the shiny red bus. It was just the Christmas present I'd always wanted.

Soon, most of the village children were outside braving the chill weather and we spent a wonderful day on the deserted bus playing at being the bus driver, conductor and passengers. We used pieces of torn newspaper for bus tickets and my gran's worn, leather shopping bag to keep them in. Nobody quarrelled or argued, we took it in turns to be in charge and had to be dragged indoors for our Christmas dinners.

Parents appeared occasionally to beg their offspring to come home to meet visiting relatives or to sing carols but it was no use. The deserted bus was the best gift we children could have hoped for.

We were unable to tear ourselves away from it…

When dusk fell it was sad to leave our freezing cold, giant Christmas present. We picked up the odd scrap of paper from the floors and swept through with a dustpan and brush. Suddenly it was as if we had never been there. The deserted bus had an air of melancholy about it as we slid our way on the crisp, icy path back into our cosy, warm home.

After the pain of defrosting cold hands and feet in bowls of warm water and having our circulation restored by being briskly rubbed with rough towels, it was time for me to settle back on the old leather chair and read

November 2008

Saturday

1
All Saints' Day

Sunday

2
London to Brighton Veteran Car Run

Monday

3

Tuesday

4
Yours magazine on sale

Wednesday

5
Guy Fawkes' Night

Thursday

6

Friday

7

Saturday

8

Sunday

9
Remembrance Sunday

Monday

10

Tuesday

11
Armistice Day

Wednesday

12

Thursday

13

Friday

14

Saturday

15

Sunday

16

Monday

17

Tuesday

18
Yours magazine on sale

Wednesday

19

Thursday

20

Friday

21

Saturday

22

Sunday	Thursday
23	27
Monday	Friday
24	28
Tuesday	Saturday
25	29
Wednesday	Sunday
26	30

PIC: REX FEATURES

Born this month

Singer Petula Clark, famous for her chart-topping hit Downtown in 1964, was born on November 15, 1932.

Married this month

Queen Elizabeth II married Prince Philip, Duke of Edinburgh on November 20, 1947.

Died this month

Handsome leading man Cary Grant (pictured) died on November 29, 1986, aged 82. His real name was Archibald Alexander Leach but changed he it to Cary Grant when he moved to Hollywood in 1931.

A Grand Day Out

George (right)
enjoying a day at Bognor

This is myself and my small friends and their parents taken around 1945 on a cold day out to Bognor beach, beach huts in the background and wearing our black trench coats – so fashionable around that time.

George Thayer, Kirriemuir, Angus

Superfood!

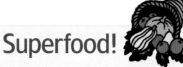

EAT MORE... SWEET POTATOES

Packed with...

Vitamins C and E, phosphorus, calcium, potassium, folic acid, magnesium and beta-carotene.

Good for...

Detoxing the body, soothing inflammation in the digestive tract and boosting circulation.

Get more by...

Roasting on the bonfire wrapped in tinfoil. Split and serve with a dollop of crème fraîche and freshly ground pepper.

TOP TIP

If your nails are dull from overuse of nail varnish, slice a fresh lemon in half and push your nails in for a few minutes. The natural shine and colour will come back.

Joanne Wilkinson, Sheffield

Great gardening

Tulips

Autumn's the best time to plant spring-flowering bulbs. Most benefit from going in during September, but tulips prefer being left until November. Although the variety 'Lady Jane' has been around for several years, it's relatively unknown and deserves wider recognition. Like all tulips, it originated in Iran and the Himalayas, but is unique, producing petals which are ivory on the inside and soft pink on the outside – these contrast prettily with the deep brown stamens. It thrives in borders, rockeries and containers – try planting it among the metallic leaves of thyme 'Silver Posie.'

■ It's available from www.qualitydaffodils.co.uk, or R A Scamp, tel: 01326 317959

AROUND THE HOUSE

Keep a list of useful telephone numbers – doctor, dentist, plumber, electrician etc – on the kitchen noticeboard, and another by the phone.

In the kitchen

■ BONFIRE NIGHT BANGERS FEAST ■

Serves 4

- 4 traditional sausages
- 1 whole garlic bulb
- 1 eating apple, cut into wedges and cored
- ¼ pumpkin or butternut squash, peeled and cut into thin wedges
- 2 large sprigs fresh rosemary
- 30 ml (2 tablespoons) olive oil
- 30 ml (2 tablespoons) maple syrup
- Foccacia bread

1 Toss together the sausages, garlic bulb, apple, pumpkin or butternut squash, rosemary, olive oil and maple syrup.

2 Bake in oven for 40-50 minutes until sausages are golden brown and pumpkin (or butternut squash) is soft.

3 Warm foccacia bread in oven and remove.

4 Squeeze the cooked garlic from the cloves and spread onto the bread. Pile everything else on to the bread, drizzle with any juice and serve as a large 'sharing sandwich' making sure everyone gets a bit of everything! Alternatively, cut into wedges and serve with chutney or dips.

Recipe courtesy British Sausage Week

We remember when...

The joy this week in 1989 as people were finally allowed to travel freely between East and West Germany. For nearly three decades the Berlin Wall had divided the two countries but after the collapse of East Germany's government, jubilant crowds converged on crossing points and clambered over the wall. In 1990, East and West Germany once again became a united country.

My childhood home

Mary on camp in 1949

I was born in 1946 on a smallholding in Leechpool, in Monmouthshire, but when I was two years old, my parents were given notice to quit. We were re-housed in the huts of the nearby Ifton Hill Army Camp, Portskewett. Since these had been vacated by the army, they were used to help tackle the post-war housing shortage.

My parents were fortunate to be given an officer's hut, which meant we had our own lavatory adjoining the hut.

The front door opened into the living room, but my Father put up a corrugated tin partition, which he painted yellow. He cut a door in it starting six inches above the door, so there were fewer drafts, and we had a hallway before entering the living room.

He hoped to start a small shop but was refused permission. However, he kept stocks of all sorts of things such as shoe laces and chocolate bars and people used to come and knock at the door to buy them.

An electricity supply was available from a generator housed at the camp entrance, which had to be started each evening at dusk. My father had the job of starting it, and was paid seven shillings and six pence a week, which just covered our rent.

There was a great sense of camaraderie on camp, and on bonfire night, we'd all pool resources and have a big firework party. One year my sister and I had whooping cough, and I can remember us sitting on little chairs, while my auntie stood outside the window, making patterns for us with sparklers.

I discovered years later that my mother hated living in the hut but as a child, I thought it was wonderful.

I was sorry when the time came to leave and we were re-housed in a council house in the village of Caldicot.

Mary Rooney, Caldicot, Monmouthshire

In the kitchen

▓ THE CLASSIC CHOCOLATE CAKE ▓

Serves 8

For the cake
- ■ 125 g (4½ oz) butter
- ■ 175 g (6 oz) unrefined golden caster sugar
- ■ 175 g (6 oz) unrefined light muscovado sugar
- ■ 2 eggs
- ■ 225 g (8 oz) plain flour
- ■ 50 g (2 oz) cocoa powder
- ■ 1 teaspoon baking powder
- ■ ½ teaspoon bicarbonate of soda
- ■ 250 ml (8 fl oz) sour milk or buttermilk

For the icing
- ■ 300 g (11 oz) unrefined golden icing sugar, sieved
- ■ 2 teaspoons cocoa powder, sieved
- ■ 15 g (½ oz) butter, melted
- ■ 2-3 tablespoons boiling water
- ■ 50 g (2 oz) plain chocolate, coarsely grated

1 Grease and line base of two 22 cm (8 inch) round cake tins. Preheat oven to 180°C, 350°F or Gas Mark 4.

2 Put butter and sugars into a bowl and beat together with electric whisk until light and fluffy. Add eggs, beating well.

3 Sieve flour, cocoa, baking powder and bicarbonate of soda into mixture, pour in soured milk or buttermilk. Stir until smooth and spoon into prepared tins. Bake for 20-25 minutes until just firm.

4 Cool in tins for 5 minutes, then turn on to a wire rack to cool.

5 Sieve the golden icing sugar and cocoa into bowl, pour in the butter and 2 tablespoons boiling water. Stir until smooth.

6 Spread half of the icing on to the base of one chocolate sponge, sandwich together with other chocolate sponge. Spread remaining icing over the cake, using palette knife dipped in hot water. Sprinkle over grated chocolate to decorate.

Recipe courtesy Billington's and Allinson

A Grand Day Out

PIC: STEVE MAISEY/REX FEATURES

A couple of years ago I went for a wonderful day out on the Flying Scotsman – what a grand old girl she is!

We boarded the train at York station, which was packed with people waiting to see us off.

I was in a carriage with small windows that opened across, and a table that seated four; some carriages had long seats with mirrors overhead, and belts on the windows.

We all felt like royalty as we chugged along, and people were taking photographs all along the line. I opened a window and got soot in my eye, just as I remembered doing as a child.

After an hour's stop for refreshments, we made our way back to the train. By this time it was nearly dark, so perhaps the journey back was not quite so thrilling but, being a railwayman's daughter, just travelling on the Scotsman was enough.

Gwen Shaw, Halifax

We remember when...

The controversial novel Lady Chatterley's Lover sold out on the very first day of its UK release on November 10, 1960. The novel, by D H Lawrence, had been banned in the UK since it was first published in 1928 due to its explicit sex scenes, but after a court case the ban was finally lifted. It went on to sell two million copies that year!

▓ TOP TIP

Always carry a carrier bag in your handbag, so if it rains, you can put your wet umbrella into the bag when you go into shops, so it doesn't drip everywhere.

Jean Mortimer, Gretna, Dumfries and Galloway

Superfood!

Packed with...

Soluble and insoluble fibre, polyunsaturated fats, protein, iron, B vitamins, vitamin E, calcium, potassium, magnesium and silicon.

Good for...

Keeping you regular! Plus, can lower your levels of 'bad' cholesterol, LDL, and can help keep your heart healthy. Also a great source of slow-release energy, which can help regulate sugar metabolism.

Get more by...

Mixing up your own nutritious muesli, adding blueberries, almonds and raisins. Also use in homemade stuffing and to thicken stocks and soups.

AROUND THE HOUSE

A cup of hot water with two teaspoons of cider vinegar in makes an effective decongestant for a cough. And for a sore throat, try hot lemon juice and honey – still the best tried and tested remedy.

Great gardening
Vanda orchid

The Vanda orchid is one of the world's most beautiful orchids – its family is one of the few in cultivation to contain orchids with blue flowers. It's as exotic as it looks, but is always worth growing – once you've succeeded, you'll be hooked! Naturally found in the Himalayas, Australia and parts of New Guinea, vandas are epiphytic (they grow on trees where their aerial roots absorb moisture in the air). Thriving on diffuse sunlight, they should be placed near a window and should never be allowed to dry out completely until they've flowered – then they can have a few weeks rest.

My childhood home

This picture is of my wonderful grandmother Mari Farrance of Bridgwater, Somerset, with nine of her 11 children, the youngest of whom survives at 90.

She lived at Escott House for most of her life, and as it was a large house, we lived here also with my cousin and his family.

The lawns were often covered with masses of Boy Scouts and Cubs as my grandparents were Commissioners for Somerset. My grandmother often had parties when all her seven sons came home on leave from the war; we had a very happy childhood with all these aunties and uncles.

Jeanne Hoare-Matthews, Weston-super-Mare, Somerset

Top: Jeanne's wonderful Granny
Above: Escott House, Bridgwater

My childhood home

My parents' bungalow was situated in a cul-de-sac close by Ashford Recreation Ground, Middlesex, ideal for walks. Newly built, Dad created a lawn and flowerbeds in the back garden, for my pram.

I was born there in November 1936, in my Rosary Gardens home at 8.45pm, Dr Pickett and Nurse Cheer in attendance. Mother was taken ill soon afterwards, so we went to live at grandma's house, Applegarth.

It was spring when we went home, and I was able to sleep in my pram in the garden. I can clearly remember sitting in my highchair, watching Mother ironing in the living room, also playing with saucepan lids in the kitchen.

My Father's job moved to Sunningdale so we went to live in a flat, over the grocer's shop, and our bungalow was let.

**Priscilla Odell,
Hampton, Middx**

Above: Rosary Gardens, Ashford, below: The house purchase receipt, 1934

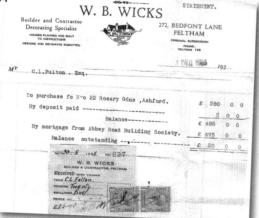

We remember when...

The National Lottery launched in Britain, this week in 1994. The jackpot was £7 million and eight people won £800,000 each in the first draw! The live lottery show was hosted by Noel Edmonds, Anthea Turner and Gordon Kennedy. The lottery is still going strong and has raised more than £19 billion for good causes.

In the kitchen

▮ SPINACH AND SQUASH FRITTATA ▮

Serves 4 – 6
- ■ 1 tablespoon olive oil
- ■ 350g (12oz) diced butternut squash
- ■ 1 red onion, sliced
- ■ 1 clove garlic, crushed
- ■ $^{1}/_{2}$-1 teaspoon dried chilli flakes
- ■ 1 x 235g (approx 8oz) bag young spinach leaves, washed
- ■ 6 large eggs
- ■ 50g (2oz) low fat cheddar-style cheese

1 Heat the oil in a non-stick frying pan. Add the squash and onion, and sauté for 4 minutes, or until pale golden. Cover the pan with a baking tray and continue to cook over a low heat for 5 minutes until the squash is tender.

2 Stir in the garlic and chilli, then add half the spinach and cover again. Cook for 1 minute until the leaves have wilted. Add remaining spinach in same way. Uncover. Season to taste.

2 Beat the eggs until smooth, then add to the pan. Cook over a low heat for about a minute until the eggs are beginning to set. Shake the pan to level the surface and cook for a further 4 minutes. Scatter over the cheese and pop under a hot grill for a further 2 minutes or until the top is set and pale golden. Serve in wedges.

Recipe courtesy Lion Quality Eggs

TOP TIP

To keep your biscuits fresh, place two or three sugar cubes in the bottom of the tin.

Mr C Symms, Stoke-on-Trent, Staffs

Great gardening

Takanini

Although the camellia 'Takanini' was bred in Auckland, New Zealand and first recorded in 1987, it has only appeared in the UK recently. With deep plum-red, anemone-like flowers and a vigorous, upright, it's highly recommended by the specialists at Trehane Nursery. However, what really makes it stand out is its long flowering period – it begins in December and may still be in flower in April.

■ To order visit www.trehanenursery.co.uk

▓ AROUND THE HOUSE ▓

Most people keep a torch handy for emergency power failures, so why not go green and use one that doesn't need batteries, such as a wind-up one.

Superfood!

▓ EAT MORE... LEMONS ▓

Packed with...

Potassium and vitamin C.

Good for...

Reducing the symptoms of osteoarthritis and rheumatoid arthritis and dissolving gallstones. Their antiseptic qualities also offer some protection against mouth ulcers, coughs, colds and sore throats.

Get more by...

Adding to salads, sorbets, marmalades and cakes or combining with olive oil, crushed garlic and ground pepper to make a salad dressing with a zing.

A Grand Day Out

Below, left: Frances and Robert ready for the off
Below, right: Brother and sister on a sunnier day 55 years later

When my brother Robert and I were small in the 1950s, money was in short supply but my Mum's imagination was not. She found ingenious ways of keeping us amused, and one wet day she gave us a day out which I often remember when it rains.

Our destination was a secret but we were going to take a picnic. She sent me to the corner shop to buy some luncheon meat which was sliced up on the bacon slicer as I waited. Sandwiches, orange juice and buns packed up in one end of the pram, and Robert wrapped up in the other.

As I splashed through the puddles, I realised we were going to the Rec! It was usually crowded but today we'd have it to ourselves, Mum explained. We went on the swings time after time, when normally we'd have to queue; see-saws, roundabouts, swingboats, we tried them all. Even Mum had a go, explaining that the ban on over-14s did not apply on wet days!

We retreated to the wooden shelter for our sandwiches and Mum got on with her knitting while we went back for a last go on everything.

At home, the fire and paraffin stove was lit to dry our clothes and kettles boiled for a wash.

**Frances Williams,
Basingstoke**

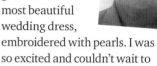

Great gardening
Dewey Blue

It's hard not to be swayed by the ethereal beauty of grasses. As they've increased in popularity, several more unusual varieties have become available and new varieties have been introduced from abroad. One of the most recent to reach our shores is Panicum virgatum 'Dewey Blue' which hails from the coastal dunes of America. A drought-tolerant plant, it produces clumps of intense blue leaves and airy panicles of flower in summer – these last well into the winter months and look magical when covered by frost. Height 1.5m.

■ To order plants, tel: 01202 873 931 or www.knollgardens.co.uk

A Grand Day Out

When I was six years old in 1947, my Mother said she was going to take me on a special trip. We were going to the city Museum in Bristol to see the Queen's wedding dress.

The Queen had married Prince Phillip on November 20, and I had cut out all the pictures I could find, and pasted them into a scrapbook.

We arrived at the Museum and there in a big glass case was the most beautiful wedding dress, embroidered with pearls. I was so excited and couldn't wait to tell my Dad all about it.

Diane Clarke, Bristol

We remember when...

Margaret Thatcher formally resigned this week in 1990, after 11 years as Prime Minister. She was the first female Prime Minister and her right-wing views brought her as many critics as it did admirers. But her reign held strong through the miners' strikes, the introduction of the hated poll tax and the Falklands War.

AROUND THE HOUSE

To keep your car windscreen frost-free, rub it with a mixture of three parts vinegar to one part water the night before.

Superfood!

EAT MORE... OLIVE OIL

Packed with...

Viatmain E, monounsaturated fat and antioxidant polyphenols.

Good for...

Protecting against heart disease by controlling LDL ('bad') cholesterol levels while raising HDL ('good') cholesterol levels. Its protective function also has a beneficial effect on ulcers and gastritis and can lower the incidence of gallstone formation. Thought to help reduce the risk of colon cancer too.

Get more by...

Using in homemade salad dressings, adding to mash potato or blending with garlic and your favourite beans to make a tasty dip that's perfect with slices of raw vegetables.

In the kitchen

STICKY TOFFEE PUDDING

Makes 6

- 75 g (3 oz) pitted dates, roughly chopped
- 75 g (3 oz) mixed dried fruit
- ½ teaspoon bicarbonate of soda
- 75 g (3 oz) dark muscovado sugar
- 75 g (3 oz) light muscovado sugar
- 75 g (3 oz) butter
- 2 medium eggs, lightly beaten
- 175 g (6 oz) wholemeal self-raising flour

Toffee Sauce

- 125 g (4 ½ oz) butter
- 175 g (6 oz) light muscovado sugar
- 60 ml (4 tablespoons) double cream
- 25 g (1 oz) pecan nuts, roughly chopped

1 Preheat oven to 200°C, 400°C or Gas Mark 6. Grease and base line 6 x 250 ml (9 fl oz) cups or pudding moulds.

2 Put dates, fruit and bicarbonate of soda into a jug. Pour on 175 ml (6 fl oz) boiling water.

3 Put the dark and light muscovado sugars into a bowl with the butter. Use an electric mixer to cream together until light and fluffy. Gradually beat in the eggs, sift in the flour and fold in the fruit mixture.

4 Spoon into prepared cups or pudding moulds. Put into a roasting tin, half fill with boiling water, then cover entire tin with foil. Bake for 30 minutes until puddings are risen firm, yet springy.

5 For the sauce, put the butter, light muscovado sugar and cream into a pan and heat gently, stirring until sugar is dissolved.

6 To serve, upturn puddings onto serving plates, drizzle over the toffee sauce and sprinkle with pecan nuts. *Recipe courtesy Billington's and Allinson*

My childhood home

Whitemoor Lodge in the winter

I was born in Nottingham at Bobbers Mill, on the Nuthall Road, in a house called Whitemoor Lodge. Sadly, this wonderful house has now been pulled down, a small housing estate in its place. But what memories of the wonderful setting to grow up in…

The house had a porch with windows both sides and a red tiled floor. My sister, Zoe, and I slept in there in our prams when the weather was bad.

The front door had stained glass leaded panels – and the one over the door knob was broken, so our cats used to jump in and out of the house this way.

On the far wall of the dining room were French windows and a large locked showcase, with memorabilia of my great-great-grandfather – his horse's tail in a silver mount, his father-in-law's Waterloo medal and other of his medals, his rifle and regalia and silver whistle on a chain – which are now housed in Nottingham Castle Museum. Near the bay window was an oak gate-legged table with four matching chairs, which are now in my home.

The drawing room was my favourite, with a grey/green Wilton carpet and French windows which opened on to the garden. There was a large mahogany sideboard with lion's head handles, a table with lion's claw feet, and mahogany chairs. We had a purple sofa and armchairs and a Steinway piano which had gold candle holders.

We all loved this house and I have never forgotten it, even though I only lived there until I was seven years old.

**Mary Fay Jones,
Chatham, Kent**

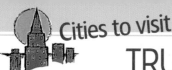

TRURO: ANCIENT AND MODERN

Beloved by Betjeman

Unlike the medieval cathedrals in many cities, Truro's cathedral is less than a century old. The foundation stone was laid in 1880 by Queen Victoria and the building was completed 30 years later. Today, its distinctive three towers dominate the Cornish county town. Viewers of the BBC's A Seaside Parish are familiar with the building as the seat of the endearingly ebullient Bishop Bill Ind, a frequent visitor to the parish of Boscastle.

Cornwall is known for its mild climate so it is not surprising that Truro is studded with beautiful parks and gardens. The Victoria Gardens beside the River Kenwyn boasts fine displays of exotic plants as well as a bandstand where concerts are held on Sunday afternoons during the summer.

Truro's elegant Georgian architecture dates back to the eighteenth century when wealthy mine-owners and merchants built grand town houses and attended balls held at the Assembly Rooms. The poet John Betjeman knew Truro well and was particularly fond of Walsingham Place, a tranquil Georgian

terrace tucked away near Victoria Place.

By contrast, Truro boasts an award-winning contemporary building in the form of its Crown Courts built on the site of the old castle and opened in 1998. More recently, Lemon Quay has been developed to provide a pleasant riverside area with shops and restaurants.

Another innovation for this ancient city is its pre-Christmas celebrations which include the City of Lights parade, first held in 1996. Every November, thousands of visitors come specially to see the amazing giant lanterns created by local artists, aided by schools and community groups.

Milk from the churn

No doors were locked where Christine Catherall grew up near Bolton

Our village

Ours was not a typical country village but consisted of rows of stone terraced cottages built in 1862 to house the workers at the Eagley cotton spinning mills. My Father was a cotton spinner and Mother worked in the canteen helping to prepare lunches for the hungry workers.

In our community everyone knew each other and no doors were locked. It was safe to let children ramble with friends around the area. We would set off with a jam butty and a bottle of water and be gone all day. Sometimes my friend

and I would make a tent out of Mum's wooden clothes maiden draped with a blanket. We'd camp out in the garden until bedtime but were never brave enough to stay out all night. In autumn we looked forward to collecting acorns and conkers. The highlight was collecting wood and old furniture for our enormous bonfire on the fifth of November.

Our milk was delivered by the farmer from his horse and cart – the milk being ladled from the churn straight into the jug waiting on the doorstep. Each week the coal man called with

his lorry. The lamplighter would come round to check all the gas mantles in the street were lit.

'Rags and bone, any cream stone', was the call of the rag and bone man who exchanged a soft, cream stone for unwanted items. Mum used the stone to whiten the edges of the doorsteps after mopping.

I still live on Eagley Bank, in a bungalow built on the land where Dad had his allotment. While digging in the garden I unearthed a glass handle that had been on the old chest of drawers he used to store items in. What memories it brought back!

Injections, frogspawn and semolina pudding

Brenda Murray doesn't like milk puddings – but we'll let her tell you why...

Slap! Slap! A firm hand was being applied to my bare, up-ended bottom as I crouched on the stiffly made bed. I sniffled and glared through slitted eyelids at my attacker. How I hated her, this tartar in her spotless uniform and starched headdress who held everyone in a perpetual state of terror.

She was the ward sister of the sanatorium where I was receiving treatment for TB, and right at that moment, it wasn't very good treatment. I pulled the bedspread over my head to blot out the angry face hovering over me. It also blotted out the lecture which I now knew by heart.

The year was 1947 and I was eight years old; my Mother was also in the sanatorium on the floor below. Meals were basic and the cooking left a lot to be desired.

I'd always been a sickly child and very picky with food. My main hates were for milk puddings, which, in the sanatorium usually consisted of tapioca (generally known among us kids as frogspawn) or semolina, always containing lumps of dry powder where it hadn't been mixed thoroughly.

I tried various means of not eating these obnoxious desserts. I bribed other young patients by swapping them for the things they didn't like and I did, and

PIC: GETTY IMAGES

I tried various means of not eating

when this failed, I squashed the revolting mess between the empty pudding bowls. Eventually, I was found out when the kitchen staff were unable to separate the dishes which had become firmly glued together because the mixture had set like wallpaper paste.

I devised a new tactic. The dining room doubled as the schoolroom and when the school holidays began the blackboard was taken down and pushed out of sight in a corner. I sat and dawdled through dinner until everyone had gone back to the ward and there I was left under strict orders to finish my pudding. Making sure no one was around,

I scraped the offending mess behind the piano, knowing that it wouldn't be used for weeks.

This plan worked well until the holidays ended and the blackboard was retrieved ready for lessons to begin the next day. My crime was then discovered and the board was now streaked with dried pudding which had set like concrete.

A new blackboard had to be ordered and I was really for it especially, as the day before, I'd scraped my dinner over the balcony narrowly missing the aforementioned Ward Sister as she returned from a visit to the hairdresser!

I've never tasted tapioca or semolina pudding since.

Brenda as a child

A MERRY LITTLE CHRISTMAS

BY LINDA LEWIS

Alice's first Christmas as a widow is bound to be a sad one – or is it?

It was the night before Christmas and John and Lynne weren't looking forward to it one little bit.

"It's going to be even worse than usual," sighed Lynne as she pushed a thick jumper into her case, "I wonder how your Mum will cope?"

"I don't know. It's going to be hard, her first Christmas without Dad."

"Do you think she'll put the heating on? Last year we could scrape ice off the inside of the bedroom window."

John patted her arm. "I wouldn't count on it. Old habits die hard. Right, checklist. Thermal underwear."

"Check."

"Emergency packet of chocolate digestives."

"Check."

"Bottle of sherry and two plastic beakers."

"Check."

Lynne giggled. "I feel like a naughty schoolgirl, smuggling alcohol into the bedroom. But Christmas isn't Christmas without a drink is it?"

"With Dad being a strict teetotaller, what else were we expected to do?"

"It's not right, dreading Christmas like this," Lynne groaned, "maybe we could ask your Mum to come to us next year?"

"We'll do that. Now come on, chin up. We have to try and look cheerful. It's traditional."

Lynne laughed. "Plenty to drink and too much food, that's traditional. Not sitting round in the gloom, drinking tea, hoping your Dad will give in and put the light on. Just for once it would be nice to

'Now come on, chin up'

have a proper Christmas dinner."

John chuckled: "Remember last year?"

"How could I forget – two slices of chicken, five sprouts, a soggy roast potato and gravy you could see through."

"Mum had to manage on a tight budget."

"You mean your Dad didn't give her enough housekeeping."

"Anyway, next year will be different. Meanwhile, let's try and make the best of it." John clicked the catch on the suitcase.

"We'll make an early start. Your folks make such a fuss if we're late."

"There's plenty of time. Anyway, it was Dad who was the punctuality nut."

She sighed then leaned over to place a kiss on his cheek. "Do you think your Mum will be okay? It won't be easy for her."

"Which is why we have to try extra hard. Never mind, in 72 hours it will all be over and we'll be back home. Snug and warm."

In her house on the other side of town, John's Aunt Cynthia had reached a decision. "This is it," she told her glass of wine, "this is the last time I'm going to my sister's for Christmas."

She picked up the photograph from her bedside table and hugged it close to her heart. It was six long years since her husband died but she had wonderful memories to keep her going.

"We had some good times, didn't we, love?" she said to the photo as she slipped it into her suitcase. They had shared some magical holidays; her mind drifted back to the Taj Mahal

Christmas was going to be different

Tim Sharville.©om

by moonlight, sunrise over the Sphinx, the view from the Eiffel Tower.

She sighed and took another sip of wine. "Now don't go getting all maudlin," she told herself sternly, "You had lots of happy Christmases when Ted was alive. Now Alice needs you. God knows, she hasn't got much in the way of happy memories to keep her going. Best holiday she and Stan ever had was two weeks in Blackpool."

She closed the case, then got into bed and switched off the light. "Soon be over," she told herself.

At number ten Acacia Avenue Alice Smith sat in front of the newly installed living flame gas fire, drinking a glass of port. Stan never allowed alcohol in the house so drinking it made her feel deliciously decadent. As she sipped, she looked round the room and wondered if she might have gone just a little bit over the

top with the decorations.

They'd never had Christmas lights inside the house, let alone outside. Stan thought they were a waste of money and a bit common. He'd have hated the giant sleigh racing across the front lawn. And the tree was so big she'd had to ask her friendly neighbour, Paul, to help put it into a large bucket filled with sand.

As she thought of Paul, she smiled. She hoped to be seeing a lot more of him in the months to come.

Alice turned her thoughts to the following day. Mentally, she checked off her list. Large turkey already defrosted. Bottles of white wine cooling in the fridge and a case of red in the sideboard. Plenty of games in a pile by the television.

She snuggled down in the comfy chair she'd bought after Stan died.

She'd loved him once and believed he'd loved her in his own way, but she couldn't help wishing he'd mellowed a bit as he grew older. Especially at Christmas. John and Lynne never said much, but she knew they hated their visits. And Cynthia? Her sister had stayed in some of the best hotels in the world. What must she have thought? It must have felt like being in an old-fashioned boarding house: no central heating, 40 watt bulbs in every room, scrappy food.

She looked round the cosy room. Things had certainly changed. And next year? She rather fancied a Christmas cruise – somewhere more exotic than Blackpool. Maybe her sister would come along for company.

Sighing contentedly, she poured another drink. One thing was for sure, Christmas was going to be very different from now on.

Monday

1

Tuesday

2   Yours magazine on sale

Wednesday

3

Thursday

4

Friday

5

Saturday

6

Sunday

7

Monday

8

Tuesday

9

Wednesday

10

Thursday

11

Friday

12

Saturday

13

Sunday

14

Monday

15

Tuesday

16   Yours magazine on sale

Wednesday

17

Thursday

18

Friday

19

Saturday

20

Sunday

21   Winter Solstice

Monday

22

Tuesday

23
....

Wednesday

24
....

Thursday

25
Christmas Day
....

Friday

26
Boxing Day
....

Saturday

27
....

Sunday

28
....

Monday

29
....

Tuesday

30
Yours magazine on sale
....

Wednesday

31
New Year's Eve
Hogmanay
....

PIC: REX FEATURES

Born this month

Television presenter Carol
Vorderman, best known as co-host
of Channel 4's Countdown, was
born on December 24, 1960.

Married this month

Well-loved actress Helen Mirren
(pictured) married American
director Taylor Hackford in
Scotland on December 31, 1997, on
his 53rd birthday.

Died this month

American rock 'n' roll pioneer
Roy Orbison, famous for hits such
as Pretty Woman and Only The
Lonely, died on December 6, 1988
from a heart attack at the age of 52.

In the kitchen

GLAZED PARSNIPS WITH SESAME SEEDS AND MAPLE SYRUP

Serves 4-6
- 700 g (1½ lb) parsnips, peeled
- 25 g (1oz) butter
- 30 ml (2 tablespoons) maple syrup
- Salt and freshly pepper
- 45 ml (3 tablespoons) sesame seeds, lightly toasted

1 Preheat oven to 230°C, 450°F or Gas Mark 8. Cut the parsnips in half lengthways and in half again. (If you're using older, tougher parsnips, cut into quarters and remove the woody cores.) Add to a pan of boiling, salted water and parboil for 2 minutes. Drain well.

2 Place the butter and maple syrup in a small pan or microwave and heat gently.

3 Transfer the parsnips to a roasting tin, then brush with the maple mixture and season to taste. Cook, shaking the pan frequently, for 30 minutes or until golden brown.

4 Sprinkle over the sesame seeds and return to the oven for 5 minutes. Transfer to a warm serving dish.

Recipe courtesy www.thinkvegetables.co.uk

TOP TIP

After watching me prick my finger on a skewer while I was rummaging in the kitchen drawer, my friend suggested I stick the ends of the skewers into a cork. I also keep a cork on the end of the corkscrew.
Mary Turner, Hebden Bridge, W Yorks

A Grand Day Out

In 2006 we had a wonderful day at Windsor, complete with a Scottish wedding in the town! Although Her Majesty the Queen wasn't expected at the castle, the atmosphere was wonderful. The traffic stopped for the Guards marching through the streets and it was a great day.
Ruby Joy Parker, Milton Keynes

Left: Marching through Windsor

We remember when...

In December 1961 the contraceptive pill became available on the NHS for the first time. It became a symbol of the sexual freedom of the sixties, although for many, there was a long way to go before sex outside marriage was accepted.

AROUND THE HOUSE

To ring the changes with mince pies, add a little ground almond to your pastry, and cut out a pastry shape – such as a festive tree – for the tops.

Superfood!

EAT MORE... DATES

Packed with...

Vitamin B3, iron, calcium and beta-carotene.

Good for...

Maintaining a healthy respiratory system and fighting against dysentery and diarrhoea.

Get more by...

Adding to cakes, muesli and flapjacks or making a sweetly tangy salad – mix together some pitted dates, chopped ham, a squeeze of lemon juice and thickly whipped cream. Serve on a bed of shredded lettuce and cucumber cubes.

Great gardening

Juncus

You won't find the juncus family in many plant encylopaedias, especially if they're a few years old. As rushes, they originate in wet regions of the world and are usually considered weeds! However, several cultivars have become popular, mainly for their twisted stems. One of the newer varieties, 'Curly Gold Strike' has golden curly lines along its spiralling leaves and stems and is extremely attractive. Plant it in moist soil in sun or partial shade.

■ You can buy it from one of Hillier's Garden Centres, or visit www.hillier.com

My childhood home

I remember the house where I was born on a cold December morning. I obligingly waited a couple of hours after Dad and my sisters left for work and school to arrive into the world with the aid of the village midwife and my gran. By the time everyone returned home, I was snugly wrapped up in the crook of my Mother's arm, with no sign of the earlier activity.

Our house was on a Monmouthshire hillside enjoying wonderful views of the surrounding hills that swept up to the Brecon Beacons in the distance. This was my home until I married in 1955 and moved away.

The large scrubbed table in the middle of the downstairs room was central to all our activities. During winter months, the oil lamp was carried ceremoniously from its daytime quarters on the windowsill and set down on the table.

A pleasant light shone on the table set for dinner. Afterwards we were then ready to read, write, do homework or play with our little celluloid dolls. Dad may even have found space on one corner to finish the Sunday paper crossword or fill in his football coupon.

Holly's 15th birthday in 1949

Our little cottage of pink-washed walls and red tiled roof is now unrecognisable following the passage of time and the many extensions, cement rendering and dark roof re-tiling. Nevertheless, the heart and soul of the house remains – the name Ty Bach, meaning Little House, has been replaced with Ty Syriol which, quite aptly, means Cheerful House.

Holly John, Bournemouth

In the kitchen

MINI MINCE PIES

Makes 24

- 350 g (12 oz) white plain flour
- 40 g (1 ½ oz) golden icing sugar
- 75 g (3 oz) chilled unsalted butter, grated
- 1 medium egg yolk
- 30-60 ml (2-4 tablespoons) water
- 411 g (15 oz) jar mincemeat
- Grated zest of 1 orange

1 To make the pastry, put the flour and icing sugar in a food processor and blend for 30 seconds. Add the butter and whizz until the mixture forms fine crumbs. Add the egg yolk and 2 tablespoons water and process together until combined. Knead lightly until smooth, wrap and chill for 30 minutes.

2 Line the mini muffin tins with 24 paper cases. On a floured sheet of baking parchment roll out the pastry to a 2mm thickness. Cut out rounds using a 6 cm (2 ½ in) fluted pastry cutter. Use a palette knife to lift into the paper cases. Prick the base with a fork. Cut out mini stars.

3 Mix the orange zest with mincemeat. Spoon a generous teaspoon of mincemeat into each pastry case and top with a mini star. Chill them while the oven preheats to 190°C, 375°F or Gas Mark 5. Bake pies for 12-15 minutes until pale golden.

Recipe courtesy Billington's and Allinson

AROUND THE HOUSE

Have a few Christmas cards ready written out and sealed, so you can quickly put that unexpected caller's name on the envelope.

A Grand Day Out

A nostalgic visit for Marjory, John and their two sons

My Golden Wedding anniversary was in 2001, and my late husband John and I decided to stay at an hotel overnight and treat the family to a meal, but my sons had other ideas. They stayed too and we had a great time.

After breakfast on Sunday morning, we expected to make the trip home but the boys had decided to take us back to Ealing where we were married.

We went to the church to remember that special day, and spoke to the present vicar. We then visited where we used to live, where John went to school, and the shop he used to work in. It was such a wonderful day and, now that John is no longer with me, one that I'll always remember.

Marjory Moore, Hemel Hempstead, Herts

TOP TIP

When grilling bacon for breakfast, place a piece of dry bread into the fat, and give to the birds in your garden – they love it. **R Sands, Boston, Lincs**

We remember when...

Four days of dense, freezing fog, which disrupted rail, road and air services across London and the south east, finally came to an end this week in 1952. As well as making Christmas shopping a miserable experience, the fog was so thick that it seeped into buildings too. It became known as the Great Smog of 1952 and was thought to be caused by very high levels of coal burning.

Great gardening

Calba

Many gardens lack colour during winter, but a few well-placed dogwoods can make all the difference – many have extremely colourful stems, whether red (C alba 'Spaethii' and C alba 'Aurea'), yellow (C stolonifera 'Flaviramea') or purple C alba Kesselringii). Since the plants are deciduous, these stems set the garden ablaze at this time of the year. Now a new cultivar has joined the mix. Coming from north-west USA, Cornus sericea 'Hedgerow's Gold' has the same vibrant red stems as many of its relations but also has extremely attractive leaves. While young, the leaves have a pronounced yellow margin and this becomes creamy-white with age. Prune all stems back hard in early March every three years to encourage new growth, as this has the best colour.

■ Available from Hillier Garden Centres, www.hillier.co.uk

Superfood!

||| EAT MORE... WALNUTS |||||

Packed with...

Iron, calcium, magnesium, zinc, potassium, folic acid, phosphorus and vitamins C and E.

Good for...

Improving metabolism and lubricating the digestive system. Also thought to strengthen the kidneys and lungs.

Get more by...

Getting the nutcrackers out on the run up to Christmas or adding to salads, rice dishes, ice-cream or muesli.

My childhood home

I remember the house where I was born, in High Wycombe in 1949, with very happy memories. It was a three-bedroom end-of-terrace with a brick built coal shed, and a second, outside toilet.

Although we had a bathroom, I still remember having a bath by the fire because the bathroom was so cold; all the house was fitted with lino, we never had any carpet. In the summer when the bathroom was warm, I remember Mum

Margaret's childhood home

buying a sachet of powdered bubble bath and whisking it up with a wooden spoon to enjoy a bath filled with lovely bubbles.

Mum and Dad got their first black and white television in 1953 and we'd all have to be quiet every Saturday teatime, waiting for the football results, so Dad could mark off his coupon.

We had a lovely large garden, as my Dad grew all our own vegetables and flowers. I recall helping dad with the chrysanthemums – he would put pots with straw in on top of canes to catch earwigs, to stop them eating the flowers. I had such a shock when I saw all the wriggling earwigs, and dropped and

Margaret on her Mum's lap

smashed the pot – and it made Dad laugh!

The saddest time of our lives was when Dad died - I was only 16. Mum remarried and is very happy, and still lives in the house where we all grew up with such happy memories.

**Margaret Rackstraw,
Selsey, West Sussex**

AROUND THE HOUSE

As a lighter alternative to Christmas pud, keep a packet of summer berry fruits in the freezer – or maybe you've frozen some berries left over from picking in the autumn. Buy some meringue cases, whip up some cream and put a spoonful of berries on each. Delicious!

Great gardening

Scindapsus

With beautifully marked leaves and a pretty trailing habit, scindapsus makes a great houseplant. As a tropical, climbing plant native to Southeast Asia, it does well to cope in our homes, where temperature, humidity and light levels all vary widely. But it does more than cope, it really thrives! It's excellent when trailing from a hanging basket, scrambling up a moss pole or cascading over the edge of a balcony. The most widely grown variety is S. pictus 'Argyraeus', which has heart-shaped leaves marbled with silver. Sheltered from cold drafts and direct sunshine, and given moist compost, you will have years of enjoyment. Scindapsus are widely available from garden centres, but you can learn more about these plants at www.flowers.org

A Grand Day Out

I had very happy family outings with Mum and Dad, and younger sister, Christina. We loved going to Mablethorpe on the train and we'd be prepared for all weathers.

Another memory I have is of Christina and me visiting Father Christmas at Lewis's store in 1951. We loved Christmas time and still do and it was such a highlight to visit Santa. Happy times.

Mary Waren, Leicester

Above: Mary dressed as a Christmas Cracker in 1957
Left: Visiting Father Christmas with Christina in 1951

Superfood!

EAT MORE... CRANBERRIES

Packed with...

Vitamins C and K, calcium, fibre, manganese and phosphorus.

Good for...

Helping prevent urinary tract infections and reducing bacterial adhesion to teeth and the formation of plaque.
Also thought to offer protection against stomach ulcers, cardiovascular disease and respiratory illnesses.

Get more by...

Adding to homemade breads, muffins and rice pudding or sprinkling on to porridge and cereal. Lightly toasted cranberries also make a delicious snack. And, don't forget to add a spoonful of cranberry sauce with your Christmas turkey!

In the kitchen

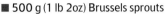

BRUSSELS SPROUTS COOKED WITH HONEY AND MUSTARD

- **500 g (1 lb 2oz) Brussels sprouts**
- **15 ml (1 tablespoon) olive oil**
- **300 ml (approx ½ pt) vegetable stock**
- **30 ml (2 tablespoons) wholegrain mustard**
- **Salt and freshly ground pepper**
- **30 ml (2 tablespoons) clear honey**

1 Cut the Brussels sprouts in half.
2 Heat the oil in a large pan, add the sprouts and fry for 2 minutes. Remove from the heat, carefully pour in the vegetable stock and stir in the mustard and seasoning.
3 Bring to the boil, simmer uncovered for 3-4 minutes until the sprouts are tender. Stir in the honey and serve immediately.

Recipe courtesy www.thinkvegetables.co.uk

TOP TIP

Banish tarnish from silverware you don't use very often by storing them in clear, airtight polythene bags. It comes out bright and shining.

Mrs J Shaw, Kenilworth, Warks

We remember when...

The Beatles had their third Christmas number one this week in 1965 with Day Tripper/We Can Work It Out, which stayed at the top for five weeks. In Christmas 1963 they'd topped the chart with I Want To Hold Your Hand and in 1964 with I Feel Fine. The group went on to have yet another Christmas number one in 1967, with Hello, Goodbye. They are still the only group in history to have had four Christmas number ones.

My childhood home

Linda and her grandma in 1965

My grandfather bought three houses in a row in about 1919. He was a shoe repairer, grocer and pigeon fancier. The village where we lived was the close-knit community of Mosborough near Sheffield.

The house we lived in had three bedrooms but no bathroom.

Linda's Grandma and cousin Eric outside the shop in 1935

The front was a grocer's shop, originally my grandfather's until my parents took it over in 1947. The shop had a central door and on one side was the groceries, the other side for pigeon and hen food, and fishing tackle.

My Dad wore a brown smock and I can remember him standing in front of the fire playing the mouth organ between serving customers.

Around the back of the house was an outbuilding which was the cobbling shop.

The next house was my grandma's and the house on the other side, my auntie's. My brother had a shed in the large garden which he made into a little house and I spent many happy hours playing in there.

My Dad died in 1964 and the grocer's shop closed.

Mother had a coal fire up until 2005 and one story I remember was, years before she was cleaning the windows, standing on the cellar grate which gave way and down she fell.

She didn't hurt herself but was none too pleased with my Dad because he couldn't stop laughing at her when her head popped out of the coal hole!

Linda Spooner, Sheffield

In the kitchen

CHRISTMAS COOKIES

Makes 60

- 200 g (7 oz) dark syrup/molasses
- 3 teaspoons ground cinnamon
- 2 teaspoons ground ginger
- 2 teaspoons ground cloves
- $^1/_2$ teaspoon finely ground black pepper
- $^1/_2$ teaspoon salt
- 300 g (approx 10 oz) butter or margarine
- 250 g Fruisana fruit sugar
- 3 eggs
- 800 g (1 lb 8 oz) sifted plain flour
- 2 teaspoons bicarbonate of soda
- 1 teaspoon baking powder
- Grated peel and juice of 1 orange
- White chocolate, to decorate

1 Put the syrup, spices and salt and pepper in a saucepan and bring to the boil. Remove from the heat and chill.

2 Cream the butter and Fruisana until smooth. Then add the eggs one by one, whisking all the time. Add the syrup/spice mixture.

3 Mix in the flour, bicarbonate of soda and baking powder, and then the orange juice and grated peel. Divide the mixture into three parts and wrap each in cling film. Chill overnight.

4 Pre-heat the oven to 190°C, 375°F or Gas Mark 5. On a floured work surface, roll the dough to a thickness of 2 mm (⅛ inch approx). Cut the gingerbread mixture into hearts or other shapes and make a small hole in the shapes. Transfer to greaseproof lined baking sheets and bake for 8 to 10 minutes until crisp and light brown.

5 Let the cookies cool on a wire rack, then decorate with melted white chocolate. Wait for the chocolate to harden, then thread ribbon through the hole and tie it into a bow, ready to hang on the tree, or for use as tags with gifts.

Recipe courtesy Fruisana

TOP TIP

Have a few silly lucky dip gifts on the dining table to unwrap after dinner – and make one washing-up liquid. Whoever gets it, does the washing up!

Andrea Hazeldine, Greenford, Middx

My childhood home

From the age of six months, I grew up in a lovely old house, Cemetery Lodge, in Horsham Road, Littlehampton. My Father was the superintendent, looking after the cemetery, and three or four other workers.

The house had three bedrooms, a kitchen and scullery, front room and an office. I lived there until I was 18, with my parents, aunt and four brothers.

We'd play hide and seek in the cemetery and once we were so long finding my youngest brother, he fell fast asleep on a gravestone.

At Christmas, Dad's office had a decorated seven foot fir tree, and a log fire burning in the grate, and in we went to receive our presents after Christmas dinner.

The house is now a funeral directors – years ago it was out in the countryside with only a farm nearby and a mile walk to school and the shops. Now there are housing estates all round it.

Caroline Green, Littlehampton, West Sussex

Below: Cemetery Lodge, Littlehampton
Right: Brownie Caroline, aged 10

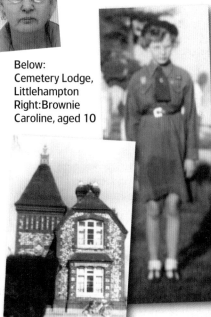

Superfood!

Packed with...

Vitamins B3, B6, C and E, folate, calcium, fibre and phosphorus.

Good for...

Lowering the risk of certain cancers, including breast, stomach and colon cancer. Also thought to help keep your heart healthy.

Get more by...

Serving with the Christmas turkey – finely slice and stir fry or roast whole in olive oil with chunks of carrots and parsnips.

AROUND THE HOUSE

Your first New Year resolution: Test your smoke alarm every week, and vacuum it out every couple of months – a build-up of dust will make it less sensitive.

Great gardening

Zamioculcas

It's the quirky appearance of zamioculcas that has endeared them to many gardeners. With strong, shiny elliptical leaves and fleshy stalks, they're certainly a complete change from the average houseplant. A member of the aroid family, they hail from Tanzania and are simple to look after, preferring to be dry rather than wet. If the lower leaves turn yellow, then you're overwatering. Zamioculcas cope admirably with quite wide variations in temperature and thrive in shade.

■ You may find them at larger garden centres, or visit www.flowers.org

A Grand Day Out

I was 16 years old when I worked at Hagenlocks Coffee Shop in Wakefield, just as the war started.

My friend Doreen and I worked such long hours but it was the day after Boxing Day and we had planned to go to Leeds, nine miles away, walking there and back.

We set out early morning, with a sandwich, arriving in Leeds about lunchtime. After a roll and soup in Lewis's cafeteria, we went off to the Grand Theatre to see a pantomime – I remember it was Tommy Trinder, then set off on the long trek home.

It was the blackout, so we had our little No 8 torches and arrived in Wakefield just in time to catch our buses home – very late in the evening with such aching feet! But we felt we'd achieved something that we'd remember over the years.

Doreen and I are both in our eighties and still good friends and we meet up several times a year.

Marjorie Britton, Wakefield

We remember when...

There were long queues outside cinemas all over the country on December 27, 1977, as thousands of people waited to see the first Star Wars film. Starring Carrie Fisher, Sir Alec Guinness and Harrison Ford, Star Wars had already taken America by storm. Who could have imagined, as we queued in the cold waiting to watch Luke Skywalker save Princess Leia from Darth Vader's evil clutches, the huge phenomenon Star Wars would become?

Cities to visit

COVENTRY: ANCIENT AND MODERN

Lady Godiva's timely show

Devastated by bombing raids in World War II, Coventry has few surviving historic buildings but instead offers visitors the many pleasures of a spacious, well-planned modern city centre – a perfect destination for Christmas shopping.

The city's chief glory is St Michael's Cathedral designed by Basil Spence. Widely regarded as a fine example of twentieth century architecture, the cathedral features the work of many contemporary artists, the most famous of which is Jacob Epstein's dramatic sculpture of St Michael's Victory Over the Devil.

Coventry's most famous citizen, Lady Godiva, can still be seen once an hour when she appears as the clock in Broadgate strikes the hour. Above her is Peeping Tom, trying to catch a glimpse of the naked lady on horseback. A more romantic depiction of Lady Godiva can be seen in a Pre-Raphaelite painting by John Collier on display in the city's Herbert Art Gallery and Museum which has recently undergone a major new development with the addition of a new wing.

In 1896, Daimler produced its first motor car in Coventry and Triumph motor cycles appeared soon after. From these beginnings grew a flourishing vehicle manufacturing industry that is celebrated in the Coventry Transport Museum.

One building that miraculously survived a direct hit from a bomb is Ford's Hospital in Greyfriar's Lane. Although severely damaged, it has been faithfully restored using original material salvaged from the ruins wherever possible. One of the city's oldest streets, Spon Street, has been preserved as a heritage area with many of its buildings carefully restored.

Stirring up the Christmas pud

Jamie Oliver would give the thumbs up to Mary Butlin's school dinners

Our village

I started school in 1949 in Staffordshire. There was only one school in the village where you went aged five and left at 15. Particular attention was paid to our handwriting and mental arithmetic – there were no calculators in those days. The girls had sewing lessons and we learned to make our own clothes by hand (there was only one sewing machine available).

There was an orchard in the school grounds; every autumn the apples were picked and carried round the classrooms for us all to take one. The boys had gardening lessons and the vegetables they grew were taken to the dinner ladies for use in our school meals. No chips or chicken nuggets for us, just good wholesome food that we loved. At Christmas, we were all invited into the kitchen to stir the Christmas pudding mixture.

In cold weather our caretaker, Mr Potts, used to disappear down stone steps into his boiler house to keep the boiler well stoked. We children created icy slides, only to be reprimanded for wearing out the leather soles of our shoes. As money was sparse, shoes were repaired at home by my Dad. My Mother knitted our jumpers, hat, gloves and scarves.

We always kept hens and pigs as we were lucky enough to have a large garden. Eggs were preserved, bacon hung from hooks in the large kitchen, and jams and chutneys were made and stored for the winter months.

In the 1950s life began to improve in many ways. We had our first television for the Coronation and my mother took delivery of her first washing machine. When North Sea Gas came to the village, we gazed in wonder at our cheese on toast cooking under the eye-level grill!

Christmas posers!

PIC: REX FEATURES

1 Saint Nicholas was the Bishop of Myra, an area in present day…?
A Greece
B Turkey
C Holland
D Yugoslavia

2 Who played Scrooge in the 1938 adaptation of A Christmas Carol?
A Lionel Barrymore
B Reginald Owen
C Alistair Sim
D Terry Thomas

3 How many Beatles singles were Christmas number ones in the UK?
A 1
B 5
C 4
D 2

4 Mary's Boy Child was the UK Christmas number one single in 1957. Who sang it?
A Harry Belafonte
B Johnny Ray
C Conway Twitty
D Danny Williams

5 What is the name of James Stewart's character (above) in It's A Wonderful Life?
A George Bailey
B Bill Bailey
C Clarence Bailey
D John Bailey

6 In which year was Johnny Mathis' When A Child Is Born the number one Christmas single in the UK?
A 1975
B 1977
C 1976
D 1978

7 What age was Natalie Wood when she appeared in Miracle On 34th Street?
A 8
B 10
C 6
D 7

8 Boxing Day, December 26th, was traditionally known as…?
A St John's Day
B St Stephen's Day
C St Michael's Day
D St Robert's Day

9 Which Christmas tradition did Oliver Cromwell ban between 1649 and 1660 in England?
A Christmas Trees
B Turkey
C Celebration
D Mistletoe

10 Humphrey Bogart was born on Christmas day of which year?
A 1899
B 1905
C 1900
D 1898

Answers: 1B, 2B, 3C, 4A, 5A, 6C, 7A, 8B, 9C, 10A

M. Clyne

Published by Pedigree in association with Yours
Pedigree Books Limited, Beech House, Walnut Gardens, Exeter, Devon EX4 4DH

Yours – the read of your life out every fortnight! Look out for it in your local newsagent.
Yours – Media House, Peterborough Business Park, Peterborough PE2 6EA. Tel: 01733 468000

Compiled and edited by Caroline Chadderton
Designed by David Reid
Sub-edited by Christine Curtis
Additional writing by Marion Clark, Sanchia Gorner, Katy Lamb, Sharon Reid
and gardening guru Gareth Salter

With grateful thanks to the following for recipes and pictures:
Billington's and Allinson, English Beef and Lamb Executive (EBLEX), Fruisana, Lion Quality Eggs,
Love Pork, Tate & Lyle, Tenderstem Broccoli, The English Pea & Bean Season, thinkveg, Sausage Week,
www.meatmatters.com, www.thinkvegetables.co.uk

◆ All telephone numbers, website details and dates correct at time of going to press

And special thanks to the readers who have contributed so magnificently to this Year Book by
sending in their memories, photographs, stories and tips